The secrets of success in selling

love

Nile

The secrets of success in selling

12 ways to achieve exceptional results

Nicola Cook

Prentice Hall
Business
is an imprint of

Harlow, England • London • New York • Boston • San Francisco • Toronto
Sydney • Tokyo • Singapore • Hong Kong • Seoul • Taipei • New Delhi
Cape Town • Madrid • Mexico City • Amsterdam • Munich • Paris • Milan

PEARSON EDUCATION LIMITED

Edinburgh Gate
Harlow CM20 2JE
Tel: +44 (0)1279 623623
Fax: +44 (0)1279 431059
Website: www.pearsoned.co.uk

First published in Great Britain in 2010

ISBN: 978-0-273-73009-5

British Library Cataloguing-in-Publication Data
A catalogue record for this book is available from the British Library

Library of Congress Cataloging-in-Publication Data
Cook, Nicola.
    The secrets of success in selling : 12 ways to achieve exceptional results / Nicola Cook.
        p. cm.
    ISBN 978-0-273-73009-5 (pbk.)
    1. Selling. I. Title.
    HF5438.25.C6556 2010
    658.85--dc22
                                                    2009036765

10 9 8 7 6 5 4 3 2 1
14 13 12 11 10

Text design by Sue Lamble
Typeset in 10 pt Iowan Old Style by 30
Printed in Great Britain by Henry Ling Ltd., at the Dorset Press, Dorchester, Dorset

The publisher's policy is to use paper manufactured from sustainable forests.

Contents

About the author

Nicola is a highly experienced sales professional who has 20 years of experience gathered throughout her award winning career.

Aged only 19 years old Nicola accepted a place on the American Express Travel Service graduate scheme, the youngest participant at that time. She quickly moved through the ranks and within four years held a senior position working in the City of London for the prestigious Chase Manhattan Account. Nicola splits her career into three key areas, the first working within the service sector, the second working in direct sales and the third devising and delivering sales strategy. She has worked with blue-chips such as American Express, Disney, Convergys, Iveco Ford and Procter & Gamble as well as some smaller SMEs and Start-ups before launching her first company in 2004.

This range of experience means Nicola has firsthand knowledge of how to deliver exceptional sales results, break into new markets and new geographical territories, build long-term customer relationships, work under extreme pressure and to very tight deadlines. She has personally recruited, built and managed high performing sales team in the Business to Business, Retail and Telemarketing sectors. Nicola also has managed numerous projects or built businesses which have involved designing and implementing strategy, and developing systems that simplify processes yet increase productivity and sales results.

She now manages her own consultancy firm which offers training, consultancy and executive coaching in all aspects of improving sales, leadership, customer service, management and personal development. She is also a well respected international motivational and business speaker. Her clients are diverse and range from large multinational blue-chips, banks, retailers and charities through to smaller business clients and start-up businesses.

Nicola is actively involved in a number of projects that support female entrepreneurship, as well as the development of enterprise culture and economic regeneration through sustainable business growth. She lives in the North East of England with her husband and their young son.
www.nicolacook.com

Other books by Nicola Cook

A New You – the small changes that make the biggest difference to your life

Introduction

Introduction

Strong sales results are a critical part of every successful business. Good sales skills lie at the heart of our ability to connect with our fellow human beings and every well-respected, successful person possess the ability to influence others; it's a prerequisite for success.

Are you someone who needs to successfully influence others? Perhaps in your role as a manager, business development executive, managing director or small business owner or perhaps even as a customer service adviser, or fund-raiser, or obviously if you are a sales executive or sales manager, you need to know how to sell and influence well.

Yet when you hear the word 'sales' what do you feel? Do you feel confident about influencing others and it's something you enjoy doing? Or does the idea of selling something fill you with dread and, given the choice, you would rather someone else take care of the sales?

Many people fear the word as much as they fear the idea of having to sell and this is often due to the bad reputation that salespeople have endured over the years, having been stereotyped as people with poor ethics and poor skills.

Today's successful salespeople are well organised and have developed an ultra-efficient sales process for their business model; they are highly skilled, confident conversationalists and operate with strong ethics. Yet because of negative historical stereotypes, the ability to influence others and to do so in a truly professional way has often not received the level of recognition it should.

The *art of selling* is a vital part of creating success, not just in delivering sales results but also in allowing fruitful relationships to develop that benefit both parties, leading to long-term partnerships, better business results, more personal drive, repeat business and transactions where everyone feels great about the exchange. Why? Because today's modern sales professionals understand that we have entered a new era of selling.

Have you ever stopped to think about what happens when you participate in a sales transaction? If you were to look up in the dictionary the definition of selling, what would you expect to see written there? Perhaps an explanation such as:

- 'A transaction between two parties'
- 'The seller matches the buyer's needs with the benefits of their product or service'
- 'An exchange of money takes place'
- 'to persuade or induce someone to buy something'.

Technically all of these definitions are true; however, 'selling' does not just take place at the end point of a transaction when money exchanges hands. The selling process begins long before you reach the final point of commitment, which is why today's buyers are much more sophisticated than ever before, and expect more from the sales process than the simple sales transaction. They are not always lured into making a buying decision simply by the cheapest deal on offer or the one that fulfils their basic need. They are more motivated by perception, value, service and a whole array of other expectations – which is why this new era comes with a new definition of selling.

As a salesperson your job is to *motivate your prospect into taking action.* In a normal sales scenario this would ultimately be gaining commitment from a customer to buy your product or service; however, this could also mean any time you need someone to take action as a direct result of your influence. This idea of 'motivating others' requires and involves a much more sophisticated approach to influencing others than the previous definitions of a straightforward sales transaction. In order to influence someone else you need to understand much more about the other person, their desires, their feelings, their goals as well as what motivates them as an individual. Then by using your sales skills be able to hook into these desires, goals and motivations to guide the buyer into making a commitment to taking the appropriate action.

So how do you master the art of selling and motivate others into action? You do this by **transferring your beliefs and emotions on to your prospect,** and it is this explanation that forms our new definition of successful selling.

> *Successful selling is a process of motivating someone into taking committed action, by the transference of your beliefs and emotions on to them.*

So accepting that we have entered a new era with new rules, how does the modern sales professional continue to create high levels of success in their sales?

They use secrets. These secrets are not something that some people were merely born with and others missed out on; they are hidden gems that often go untold, yet, as this special book will reveal, secrets that anyone can learn. This book unlocks these secrets and shares with you practical ways in which you can apply them, allowing you to improve *your* sales performance, *your* ability to influence others and ultimately achieve the results you truly desire.

How to get the most from this book

This book is split into three parts: first, to help you improve your own sales ability; secondly, to refine your sales skills with multiple sales tools and, finally, to demonstrate how to apply them in an ongoing winning sales strategy. Each of these elements is equally important, as exceptional sales results can only be achieved when all three are mastered and then seamlessly combined.

In Part 1 of the book we will focus on *you* and your sales ability: uncover how you perceive yourself as a salesperson and find out how you can improve your levels of self-confidence and design motivating sales goals. You will discover how to maintain your motivation particularly following rejection, and you will find out the reasons why some people seem to buy from you easily and others fob you off or never come back to you, even when they appeared initially interested.

The second part of the book uncovers the secrets of successful sales skills. Sales professionals today need to understand relationship-building skills, and how to structure and control a sales interaction whilst at the same time recognising that, due to the explosion of the internet and the ease of acquiring information, buyers today are more knowledgeable and sophisticated than ever before. Therefore, the secrets in this section will equip you with more ways of engaging, qualifying, compelling and gaining commitment from your prospects and show you how to lead a 'purposeful conversation' as well as overcome any reluctance from your buyer.

And finally, the third part of the book combines the previous elements into a winning sales strategy, designed to support your ongoing sales relationships. This will allow you to identify and cultivate your ideal prospects, develop the best use of technology for your sales process, use your time more efficiently and ultimately stay focused on achieving your desired success.

Throughout the book you will find exercises to carry out which will encourage you to take the information from the book and apply it. Therefore, I suggest you keep a notebook of your thoughts and ideas, or keep your completed exercises in a reference file. This book is designed to work as a practical companion, so carry it with you and refer back to it regularly. Make notes in the margin, or underline as you go. The more you *claim* the book as your own and the information in it, the more likely you are to use and apply the secrets from its pages.

However you choose to draw the information from the pages of this book, one thing I can guarantee is that you absolutely *won't gain any benefit unless you make a commitment to **use** these secrets*. Knowledge without action is worthless, so as you embark on reading this book, make sure you place your emphasis on what you don't know and what actions you need to take.

Whatever your starting point or level of experience, by using the information within these pages, I guarantee you will unlock the secrets of success in selling, and your sales results will improve as a result.

Free templates for each exercise are available online from my website, or to sign up for additional support with the FREE 30-day Secrets of Success in Selling Support Programme visit: **www.auroratraining.com**.

Sales secret

◆ The top *earners* are also the top *learners*: high-performing sales professionals are not just basking in their success, they constantly evaluate, not just what they do well, but also what changes they need to make in order to continuously improve. Complacency will kill your sales results.

PART 1

You and your sales ability

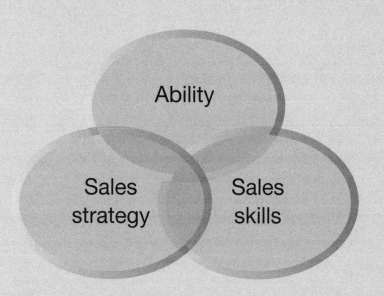

Ability

Sales strategy

Sales skills

Ability

◆ It begins with belief

◆ Flick the ON switch

◆ Tune into radio station WIIFM

◆ Why some people buy and others fob you off

Part 1 of this book is all about you and your sales ability. Before we reveal a plethora of sales skills in Part 2 that will improve your sales performance, the first four chapters will enable you to uncover your self-motivation and your desire to succeed in sales and will help you uncover ways to maintain your self-belief, particularly after you've experienced a setback.

1

It begins with belief

THERE IS A REASON you have committed to reading this book. You may already know that you need to make change and you are actively seeking ways to improve your sales performance, or perhaps you are simply curious about the *sales secrets* that others seem to naturally possess and the influence they appear to exude easily over others. Either way the first secret of successful selling is to understand the direct connection with your levels of belief and the level of your sales ability.

Belief and emotions: why they matter

If you now appreciate that successful selling is the process of motivating others into taking action through the transference of your beliefs and emotions, then first you need to clearly define the *action* you wish to induce as a result of your influence, **before** learning how you can improve your results by applying all the other sales secrets you will discover in this book.

I am always evaluating the action I wish to achieve in any given sales situation and the outcome I wish to achieve, and this may not involve gaining dollars or pounds, yet still requires the same use of my ability to influence others and therefore is still technically a sales transaction.

For example, will my outcome achieve the following:

♦ gain an appointment with a prospect;

♦ communicate a complicated piece of information with my team and have them act upon the information in some way;

♦ agree a further sales meeting with an Ultimate Decision Maker;

♦ motivate others to take more personal responsibility for their actions;

♦ execute a marketing campaign that yields a tangible result, i.e. a certain number of enquiries through our website;

♦ agree a contract with a new customer?

All of these are examples of sales influence in action, even though only the final one on the list results in income generation; they all involve motivating someone else into taking action in some way. They are all examples of successful selling. If people are not taking action as a result of your interaction with them, then you are not successfully selling to them.

If you're wondering how beliefs and emotions impact successful selling and it's not something you've considered before, let me make this absolutely clear. **You are not selling stuff; you are selling beliefs and emotion!** The products and services you offer, and the way in which they are offered, even in a corporate business context, merely allow the client to believe and feel something.

So if you thought your job was only to sell stationery, holidays, mortgages, clothes, business services, accountancy, banking, cars, cleaning products, property, mobile phones, shoes, garage doors, gadgets, pets, education, wellness, books, music, interior design, toys, bedroom furniture or any other service or product, you are sadly missing the biggest trick in the book. Highly successful salespeople know that focusing only on their product or service is only the beginning of the sales process: that in fact commitment from the buyer only occurs when they successfully fulfil much deeper emotional needs within their buyer.

> *Sales secret*
> ◆ You are selling the prospect an emotional attachment to your product or service and the belief in what owning your product or service will *feel* like to them.

Let me give you an example of how beliefs and emotions can have a negative affect on your buying choices. Have you ever received a telesales call from someone who lacked motivation or passion in their product or service? I consider telesales to be one of the hardest jobs in sales, yet very often telesales advisers are poorly paid and poorly trained so is it any surprise that this type of job is often used as a 'stopgap' before moving on to something else as opposed to a career choice and, as a result, often telesales advisers lack pride and passion in their work?

However, as a potential customer listening to this type of call, what 'beliefs and emotions' do you pick up from the salesperson at the other end of the phone? When I've asked this question in my seminars, delegates often respond with examples such as:

'Couldn't be bothered'

'Weren't interested'

'They sounded bored and apathetic'.

When I ask them what beliefs and emotions they pick up from these types of sales calls, again the delegates often respond:

'I didn't feel important'

'I didn't believe that the salesperson even believed in their product'

'I felt like I was simply the next sucker on the list and they weren't bothered whether I said yes or no'.

Is it any surprise then, that as a customer you are less likely to listen, let alone be motivated to buy? Therefore, one of the fundamental principles in successful selling is *your* ability to maintain positive beliefs and emotions.

Sales secret

◆ Your prospect will unconsciously pick up on your beliefs and your emotions, with or without your intention – so they'd better be positive!

Belief in what?

Before you can even embark on engaging with a customer, you need to ensure that you have belief in three key areas.

1 Yourself

2 Your product

3 The market opportunity

Belief in yourself

First, you **must** have self-belief and belief in your own ability as a sales professional. Everyone feels nervous and lacks confidence at certain times in their life, yet as an extraordinary salesperson you must conquer these fears and approach every situation feeling confident in your own ability. Don't panic if you know this is an area you need to work on, as we will cover *how* to do this in the next chapter.

If this sense of self-belief does not exude from within your core, your prospect will become bored very quickly, will not place the necessary level of importance on your presentation and will often dismiss your points without much consideration, and that's if you manage to get past the gatekeeper! As a professional salesperson, you will always face rejection and unless you know how to handle your own self-belief, rejection of any kind often has the detrimental effect of fuelling further feelings of inadequacy and so the vicious cycle of low self-belief continues. Therefore, before you engage with your client you absolutely must know how to flick on your own 'ON' switch.

Also, if you have an underlying low level of self-belief you are likely to miss opportunities where you could have offered a service to your client that would have benefited them in some way. You become fearful of rejection to the point that you stop selling – a guaranteed recipe for sales disaster!

Belief in your product

Secondly, you need belief in the benefits of your product or service. If you do not believe that your product delivers the benefits you sell, then you would have to be a pretty hard-nosed salesperson, or a pretty desperate one, to continue with the sale – neither of which will lead to long-term relationships with your customer, repeat business, customer referrals or the building of your brand reputation.

I was recently asked my opinion on the difference between 'influence' and 'persuasion' and although they are only words in the English language, I do think they mean different things. True influence follows our definition, where a prospect is motivated by positive beliefs and emotions to take some form of action that benefits both them and the influencer; whereas persuasion alludes to a process where the prospect is persuaded to take action that may or may not have benefit. Although they may agree to the sale, they will often feel that they have been persuaded against their will; they are more likely to develop 'buyer's remorse' and back out of the deal, and they will always associate those negative feelings with you, your product, your company and your brand.

Therefore, if you want to cultivate long-term relationships with your client base, then only offer them products or services that will benefit them.

> ### Sales secret
>
> ◆ The only difference between a *salesman* and a *conman* is their level of integrity.

In my own sales career I have left three roles (two for 'blue-chip' companies) because I felt my integrity was being compromised. Before walking away I raised my concerns with my superiors and suggested some positive changes that would have improved our service and therefore my belief in the company. Yet I was continually expected to represent the company in such ways that meant we did not live up to the expectations we had set – at one point, blatantly overcharging a customer, in order to meet our gross profit margins. This type of activity absolutely does not fit with my personal values and I certainly never wanted to be known as a 'conman'. So although some people would consider it career madness, moving on was an easy decision for me to make.

If you feel you fall into this category, first always consider how you could improve your proposition so that it does fulfil your client's needs. Perhaps you need to be realistic about the timeframes you commit for delivery or about the functionality of a particular product or service, but if you feel that in order to be successful in a particular organisation you would have to compromise your personal integrity, pack your bags and go! Preferably sooner rather than later.

Ultimately you are selling you, and what you believe about your product or service. If you compromise this, then you are selling yourself short and you will never achieve your full potential. Don't compromise here; no amount of short-

term sales results are worth sacrificing your personal
integrity for.

Belief in your market opportunity

And finally, it goes without saying that you must have belief
in your market opportunity: that there are people out there
who need and want your opportunity. Market opportunities
come and go and you need to create new opportunities and
adapt to changes in existing market conditions.

In the early stages of a new business or new business
opportunity, maintaining belief in this area can sometimes
be challenging. Good market research at the business planning stage will often build your belief in this area, and on
Day 1 of your new business venture when you're sitting in
your new office (or back bedroom as is often the case in
business start-ups) waiting for the phone to ring, you may
be feeling fairly upbeat; roll six months down the line when
all you've faced is rejection after rejection, fob-off after fob-
off and that belief may have started to wane.

Sales secrets

◆ If you don't believe there is a market for your
opportunity, stop! Even if there is, you won't make the
sale. Either reinvigorate your belief or go and find
something else that gets your juices flowing.

◆ Likewise, don't be deluded. If a market opportunity
doesn't exist, your passion alone won't create a need
where one doesn't exist. You must be able to transfer
your passion and belief into benefits that someone will
want to pay for. Being successful in sales can also be
about the timing of your opportunity.

The last employed sales role I had in my career before I started my own business was working for my good friend Michael Heppell when he was in the early phases of his business development. It was a very interesting time in my career, particularly as we were a new business which was very different from the 'blue chips' I began my career with.

We had very little in the way of resources, and certainly no marketing budget. I have never received so much rejection from a marketplace as I did in the first five months of working there! No one had heard of us; we were fairly specialised in what we offered and initially it appeared that every which way I attempted to break into the market, I bore no results.

However, what I do remember about those first few months is the amount of belief everyone in the team had – it was amazing: belief in ourselves, belief in our services and belief that someone somewhere needed us; my job was simply to keep going until I found them! In those initial months until the business started to bear fruit, we all lived on belief alone. So even though the market conditions were tough, I absolutely loved my job and wanted to keep going. This later proved to be a great foundation for maintaining belief when I started my own business in 2004.

If you lose your belief in your market for whatever reason – perhaps your sales results are falling, or everyone appears to be saying 'No, not yet' or 'Let me think about it' – then first make sure you are approaching *every* opportunity with the utmost amount of belief and skill; however, if your results still do not match up then maybe it's time to re-evaluate your marketplace and your proposition. Has the market opportunity shifted and you haven't yet responded? What are your competitors doing that has perhaps increased market expectations? Is your market simply in decline? Do you need to innovate? Or is it you? Do you lack the drive and motivation to keep pushing into a yet unproven market-place? If so, either spend some time and reacquaint yourself with the market potential or get out. It may just be time to leave and find a new sales opportunity – something that excites you and gets you leaping out of bed in the morning.

Take a moment now to complete the exercise below and score the strength of your current beliefs in the three key areas in the right-hand column, with 10 being the highest.

Score yourself between 0 and 10

Belief in yourself	
Belief in your product, service and/or company	
Belief in your market opportunity	

Strong beliefs with scores between 8 and 10 will mean that you approach every opportunity supported with strong empowered behaviours and you are already increasing your potential success with such a solid foundation.

A score between 5 and 7 will highlight the areas that you will need to work on. Perhaps there is a key issue that is worrying you at the present moment? Have you received a couple of knock-backs lately that have dinted your confidence or do you suddenly find yourself outside your comfort zone for some reason? Perhaps your company has just developed a new product which has yet to establish itself in the marketplace? If this is the case don't throw the towel in just yet: you may just need to refocus and reconnect with your core beliefs.

If you scored yourself below 5 in any of the areas, then you clearly need to take some focused action to improve your belief in whichever area needs attention. A score below 3 is a 'red flag' and cannot be left to fester as it is absolutely hampering your ability to sell and influence others. However, don't panic: the following two chapters will help you address these areas if they are a key concern for you.

What you feel, they feel

The final element of understanding how to behave in the new era of selling is to understand the transference of emotions that takes place during the sales process. As we alluded to previously in this chapter, whatever you're feeling your prospect will also feel. Empathy is part of what makes us human, so whether you intend to transfer your emotions or not, your client will unconsciously pick up on everything you're feeling. So if you feel nervous, your client will feel nervous. If you feel confident, your client will also feel that air of confidence. If you arrive at an appointment late, feeling rushed and disorganised, your client will also pick up on your agitation. Therefore, no matter what emotions you feel throughout your day, you must find ways to ensure you always approach *every* sales interaction in a 'peak state' with the ON switch flicked in the right direction; otherwise no matter how great your sales skills, you will hamper your sales potential if you cannot control your own emotional state and ensure that you approach every interaction in the best frame of mind.

Before we discuss how to manage your emotional control, over the next seven days make a note, perhaps in your diary, of how you feel 30 seconds before you engage in a sales conversation. This includes any moment when you may be connecting with an existing customer or speaking to a potential sales prospect; it doesn't matter whether it is over the telephone, in a face-to-face meeting, or even at a networking event – record how you feel. Then review your notes, and from the list below circle the emotions you feel most frequently. Add your own examples if you need to.

Circle the emotions you feel most frequently

Nervous	Excited
Worried	Empowered
Unimportant	Happy
Lacking in confidence	Proud
Alone	Fulfilled
Uncertain	Confident
Let down	Certain
Fearful (particularly of potential rejection)	You know what you are doing
Expecting the worst	Part of a team
Disorganised	Organised
Out of control	In control
Clueless	Knowledgeable

Remember, in any sales situation you are always selling yourself first; your prospect may not remember all the finer details of your sales presentation, but your presence alone will leave them with a lasting impression, and to be successful, clearly that impression needs to be positive.

> *Sales secret*
>
> ◆ People buy from people they like. And we always prefer
>   positive people with sunny outlooks to those who
>   always see the glass half empty.

When my good friend Colin – who now runs his own successful company – was employed in a sales role, he gained an
appointment with a large manufacturer of garage doors, with
the intention of selling a training programme to their sales
force. After that initial meeting the sales process progressed
and our company won the contract – the largest contract in
our organisation at that time.

When I had the opportunity to ask the HR director what it
was about that initial meeting with Colin that was so positive, he replied honestly that he couldn't hardly remember a
word that Colin had said, but he remembered his boundless
enthusiasm and belief in what we were offering; and his lasting thoughts after Colin had left were 'Flippin' heck, I wish
our sales team had that same level of passion and enthusiasm: we need some of what they have'.

That was the *secret* that won us that particular contract;
the details of *what* we were going to deliver and *how* we
would implement it were secondary to Colin's self-belief and
belief in our product, and ultimately how he transferred
those beliefs and emotions across to our potential client
secured the business.

Now you understand the new era of selling, next you need
to know how to ....

2

Flick the ON switch

YOU MAY BE A PERSON who has specifically chosen sales as a career, or you may have to influence others as part of your role but given a choice you would avoid selling like the plague, or perhaps you feel you sit somewhere between the two extremes. Regardless of your professional role, if you are going to improve your powers of influence then it's crucial to know how to sustain your levels of self-belief. Everyone has days when they are brimming with confidence and they feel they could take on the world and other days when they wish they could stay in bed and hide under the duvet! So regardless of the situation you find yourself in, you need to know how to flick your ON switch when it really matters.

Even the most talented sales professionals, if they do not have a strong confident mindset, will fail to achieve their full potential; likewise a person who may not know all of the latest sales techniques can still be very effective if they know how to flick their ON switch to the correct position.

> ### Sales secret
>
> ◆ Success is 80% right mindset and 20% right skills and know-how. Pay as much attention to your attitude as you do to your sales technique.

Flicking on that illusive ON switch is a critical part in creating your ultimate sales success. When you are switched ON you are full of belief (in all three key areas), positive emotions ooze from every pore in your body, you emulate charisma, people radiate towards you and listen to what you have to say, you improve your powers of influence and most importantly they are more likely to buy from you. Everyone has an ON switch; however, some people prefer to scrabble around in the dark, rather than learn how to switch it on when they need to. Most people find they have days when it all clicks and everything seems to come naturally; yet no matter how confident you are naturally, everyone is human and everyone has days when they are racked with self-doubt, low confidence and not much belief in their abilities as a salesperson. So if you ever find yourself in this situation, this is when you need to know how to regain control of your ON switch.

You were born to sell

When I first tell people this, most think 'How can I possibly be born to sell, have you *seen* my sales results?!'

Everyone has within them (perhaps lying dormant) a super confident salesperson just waiting to be let out. The reason I make that claim with such conviction is that everyone at one point in their life was a toddler – and toddlers happen to be amongst some of the most persuasive people in our society! Warranted their motives may be purely selfish (therefore you could say that they fit our criteria for a conman!), but if you have ever had the experience of interacting with a small child who wants something (perhaps an extra sweet before dinner, or to stay up an extra hour before bedtime), you will understand how persuasive they can be. They have no concept of rejection – they simply speak out, stating their request with the expectation it will be fulfilled and, boy, do they increase the intensity if their needs are not met immediately! They have massive powers of influence. No I'm not suggesting that to be successful in sales you need to adopt childlike behaviour to get your own way, but readopting their lack of fear of rejection may be what's needed.

The challenge with most adults, particularly those with low self-belief, is that they have lost touch with this part of themselves, instead choosing to focus on all the negative images they associate with the stereotyped salesperson – whereas the reality is that *the art of selling* is present in so many roles in our society.

Think about how all kinds of people are involved in influencing others in some form or another.

◆ A teacher who needs the attention of his pupils, in order to share his knowledge with his class.

◆ A religious leader who shares their principles and beliefs with their congregation.

◆ A parent who needs their child to adhere to the family and household standards and routines.

◆ A business leader who needs everyone to buy into the company vision and strategy.

◆ A doctor, lawyer or other professional who needs someone to follow their advice.

◆ A man who's proposing to his girlfriend. He may be using a diamond ring as a BIG incentive but she has to believe that he will offer her unending wedded bliss!

So although you may not have previously perceived yourself as a salesperson in the traditional sense, I guarantee you are already using selling skills in many areas of your life, You may just need to learn how to transfer them to your professional life, and this begins with your mindset.

Give yourself a new label

If it helps, give yourself a new job title, one that you feel reflects the qualities of the type of person you wish to emulate. Labels and how we choose to identify ourselves are very important, as they link directly with our self-image and our personal motivation.

I remember a client of mine, who simply did not feel comfortable with the job title 'Sales Executive'. Her aversion to the image of a 'salesperson' was so negative that it was holding her back. So as well as working on her associated beliefs with this image, the easiest thing to do was to change her job title to 'Business Development Executive'. The impact was instant: she immediately relaxed (her shoulders visibly dropped) and a confident smile spread across her face. She felt comfortable and confident with that label, even though nothing had actually changed in her job function; this one small difference had an impact on her results almost immediately.

Sales secret

◆ Choose your own job title, making sure the 'label' has an empowering meaning for you, something that motivates you, and makes you feel proud.

Throughout my own career I have had numerous job titles, including the obvious ones such as Sales Executive, Sales Manager and Sales Director. The less 'salesy' labels were: Area Manager, Business Development Manager, Account Manager, Customer Service Manager, and even the more recent ones of Business Consultant, Professional Speaker, Author, Managing Director and Executive Coach. However, the one thing that is common about all of these *roles* is that at their core lies the ability to influence others.

'Reject me – I love it'

This is not usually what you expect a sane human being to proclaim. Most people do not like the feeling of being rejected: yet, in sales, it will happen. Sometimes it may seem like rejection; frustration and disappointment are all you feel; so before we look at better ways of dealing with rejection, let's turn our attention to understanding more around why we feel such a *fear* against it.

One of the strongest human needs is the desire to be accepted, to be validated in some way and to connect to our fellow humans and ultimately, on some level, to be loved. Ultimately we are pack animals and we flock together in herds; we create tribes, friendship groups, bond in relationships, build cities and organisations. Therefore the idea that someone may say 'No' to something that we offer, strikes us at our very core, and continuous rejection can (if allowed to) erode the very core of our self-belief, self-perception and self-confidence. So is it any surprise that our natural instinct, almost as a form of self-protection, is to avoid rejection and avoid putting ourselves into situations where we may be exposed to it?

However, if rejection forms an inevitable part of selling, we can't avoid it; we simply need to find better ways of dealing with it, protecting our self-belief and self-confidence in the process.

Sales secret

◆ Although we use our powers of influence to affect the outcome of a situation, we can't ever truly control the responses of our prospect – only ever how we choose to react. Learning to react positively to even the most negative of situations will ultimately lead to positive results.

The key here is to disassociate any rejection you may experience in your professional role from rejection of you as a person. Just because a prospect says 'No, I don't want to buy', this does not mean that you are unimportant, worthless or even undeserving of validation, affection and connection! Yet you would be surprised how many people I work with who have a fear of rejection in their professional lives, which is ultimately linked to a fear of rejection on some level in their personal lives. They have usually experienced some form of rejection somewhere at some time in their own life (and let's face it, you would have to have had a pretty unusual life to have gone through life without ever experiencing some form of rejection!) and have cross-referenced the emotions associated with those events with some form of self-protective behaviour in their professional life, which absolutely will not help them if they need to improve their sales results.

Sales secret

◆ Accept that the client doesn't reject you personally – just your proposition.

Learning to cope with rejection is one of the biggest secrets that successful salespeople learn to overcome. You will have some days where a 'dead cert' customer turns you down unexpectedly, and unless you turn your attitude around fast you risk blowing your next opportunity. But what if the next customer rejects you too, and the next one and the one after that? **Your level of sales success is directly proportional to how well you manage your attitude, confidence and belief.**

Yeah but, no but – reclaiming your internal dialogue

All of us have a voice in our head. It is the 'gut instinct' that often drives our behaviour when we are faced with making a choice. This voice also forms part of our self-perception, how good we feel about ourselves and our ability. I call this voice the Vicky Pollard voice, as a reference to the character, made famous by Matt Lucas from the UK TV series *Little Britain*, in which the character Vicky Pollard begins every sentence with a series of 'Yeah but, no but'. This type of rambling is often what this internal voice sounds like in our mind, particularly when we find ourselves being challenged in some way or we are outside our comfort zone.

One voice is saying 'Yeah go for it, I believe in you, I know you can do it, you're the greatest', whereas the other voice is very often saying 'Idiot, you're a waste of space, who's going to buy from you, why bother, they're probably going to say no anyway'. And we are continually torn between these two opposing points of view, deciding whether to take the risk and contact the prospect, or stay within our comfort zone and protect ourselves from potential rejection.

Have you ever stopped to consider which is the more powerful voice in your own head? I guarantee that if you hold yourself back, resisting the sales risks that you know you should be making, you will have a stronger 'No but' Vicky Pollard voice. Whereas every extraordinary sales professional, who appears to be streets ahead of their competition, is fuelled by a positive, empowering 'Yeah go for it' voice. People with a strong internal voice, no matter what situation they find themselves in, no matter what rejection they may have just faced, are always switched 'ON'; they face every new sales situation with the same level of enthusiasm, self-belief and charisma.

However, no matter which voice is dominating your thinking, there is a way you can retrain it, or make it even more empowering – by using positive mantras.

A mantra is a statement that you say to yourself over and over again, and over a period of time it reaffirms your self-belief. The reason why this works so well is that our uncon-scious mind does not distinguish between what is correct or incorrect – it simply is 'just so'. Therefore if you present your mind with a positive statement over and over again which is designed to build your self-belief, and flick that magic switch to 'ON', it takes a very short period of time (around 28 days) for your new belief to drown out any nega-tive ramblings from your disempowering Vicky Pollard voice.

When designing your mantra there are four simple rules you must apply.

Make it positive. This may seem pretty obvious: if the purpose is to overpower the negative Vicky Pollard voice in your head, the last thing you want to do is give even more power to the *No buts*! However, many people don't realise the emotional intensity behind the words they use and the power they have.

Create your mantra from what I call 'moving towards lan-guage' so you state your intentions as you want them to be, as opposed to what you want to avoid feeling.

For example, take the phrase 'I don't feel stressed'. Remember that your unconscious mind does not evaluate; everything is accepted as 'just so', and therefore although the intention of the statement is to avoid the feeling of stress, by the very inclusion of the word 'stress' this actually has the complete opposite effect – it reinforces the feelings of stress! A better statement using 'moving towards lan-guage' would be 'I feel calm, relaxed and in control'. Even if when you say the mantra, you don't actually feel calm, relaxed or in control, you induce a *moving towards* frame of mind, where very quickly you will move into a state of feel-ing calm, relaxed and in control.

State it in the present tense. Using a mantra that is future-based means the results will also always be future-based. 'I will hit my sales target this month' is less powerful than 'I am achieving my sales target and goals – NOW!' When you pronounce your intentions as if they are already happening, that kick-starts your consciousness to take the action to make it happen now.

One of the strongest needs within our brains is the need to match what our ego perceives with our reality. This explains why our brains require order or at least for things to match how we perceive them. Therefore if we use a positive mantra that is different from our current circumstances, it becomes more powerful by emotionally conditioning it into our mind: by repeating it over and over, our mind works faster and drives us to match our current situation with our internal programming.

So, for example, you might say 'I have all the confidence I need within me now' (which by the way is one of my favourite personal mantras) even if at the time you initially say it you actually don't feel confident. Perhaps you're feeling nervous as you are about to walk into a very important meeting; then your mind wakes up with a lightning flash and says 'Oh OK, in order for this to be true, what do we need to do in order to feel confident; what action do we need to take?' Then your brain will release the necessary hormones to *enable* you to feel the confidence you desire.

Make it about you personally. The purpose of a mantra is to change *your* emotions and behaviour, not someone else's. So there is no point at all creating a mantra such as 'They're going to say "Yes"' or 'They need to understand me'. Oh no, no, no. All that happens when you think like this is to redirect your focus outwards to external stimulus that is beyond your control. You actually give away your power. Remember the only choice you *ever* have is how we choose to behave in response to the things that happen to us.

When a pebble is thrown into a pond, it causes a series of ripples to radiate outwards from the centre. Create a mantra that is directed towards your own behaviour and you are the pebble, create a mantra directed towards someone else's behaviour and you are the ripples, helpless against the changes that happen around you.

So always make sure your mantras are about you and what you need to change.

Say it out loud and say it proud! The final element to make a mantra truly powerful is to say it OUT LOUD! Warranted that there is a time and place for this. Perhaps in front of your client as you are about to begin your sales presentation would not be the ideal time! However, when you give life to words, by proclaiming them out loud, you intensify the emotions behind the statement; and remember how crucial emotions are. Ultimately you are your emotions. They drive your behaviour and affect your powers of influence; therefore the more emotional intensity behind your mantra the more likely you are to drown out the negative Vicky Pollard voice.

Take a moment now to write a couple of mantras that you feel would empower your own internal dialogue. What do you need to feel in order to build your own feelings of self-belief?

Here are some examples to get you started:

'All I need is within me now!'

'I am creating the best possible outcome for my client and myself'

'I am the best at what I do'

'Where others focus on obstacles I spot opportunities'

'I am the master of my own destiny'

'I always choose to respond positively to the events that happen around me'

'I am calm and in control'

When and how to use mantras. Mantras can be used in two ways to improve your sales performance. First, as a daily exercise to reprogramme any internal negative dialogue that your Vicky Pollard voice may be saying. Just as you take a shower and clean your teeth every morning to keep your physical body in tip-top condition, think of your mantra as a way of keeping your mind clean and positive. So find a way to build 10–15 minutes of time into your daily schedule when you can shout your mantra at the top of your voice. Maybe as you drive to work, or spend 10 minutes in your office with the door closed. Personally, I choose to do mine in the shower every morning: it's about the only few minutes I have every day uninterrupted on my own!

Secondly, you can use a mantra to regain your self-control in an instant if you find yourself in a particularly challenging situation either just before you enter a sales meeting, or following a rejection. The last thing you want to do is carry any negativity into your next sales meeting. Take a few moments to say your mantra, perhaps in the car, or for a few minutes outside in the fresh air, to cleanse yourself of any negative feelings and refocus your beliefs and internal feelings of confidence.

Get off your backside and move!

The final technique that will flick that magic switch to the 'ON' position is simply to 'get off your backside and move'.

Using your body to change your mood is not just some mystical theory but has been proven scientifically. When you move your body you change your internal brain chemistry, which in turn affects how you feel.

Think about it: when you feel sad, depressed or lacking in confidence, how do you hold your shoulders; how do you breathe at what angle do you hold your head; how fast do you walk? Whereas when you feel upbeat, happy or confident, how does your body movement differ?

Just like reprogramming your internal dialogue, you can change your mood just by moving in the way you wish to feel. It will only take a couple of seconds for your brain to catch up. So if you find yourself walking into a pretty intimidating sales situation and, just when you need it most, all your confidence deserts you, simply lift your head up, pull your shoulders back, take a deep breath and walk at pace and before you know it the feelings of confidence will return.

Sales secret

◆ Even those who appear at the top of their game, at some point have experienced all their confidence deserting them. The difference is simply, they have effective methods to regain it – instantly.

Break free from the confines of your comfort zone

When you start to use these belief-building techniques you will find it easier to break out from the confines of your comfort zone.

Moving beyond your comfort zone is a prerequisite when it comes to becoming a better salesperson. You have to invite challenge in order to keep growing. Remember, complacency will kill your sales results. And in my experience most salespeople can become bored very easily and need to keep challenging themselves, either by taking on more and more demanding customers, expanding their product portfolio, or breaking into new territory.

Therefore, find new ways of challenging yourself professionally, step up to the plate and volunteer when others don't, be open to new ways of learning, accept that you are an ever-evolving model that will never be finished (if you do, your shelf-life will be short), and that with every failure and rejection comes the opportunity to learn and grow as a result.

> *Sales secret*
> ◆ Every time you push beyond the self-imposed confines of your comfort zone, you increase your levels of confidence.

Chris Baxter had a high-flying career in corporate industry before he started his own business, a consultancy offering business advice and mentorship. Educated to Master's degree level, he's not short on knowledge, yet until he worked for himself, he'd never encountered the coalface of selling: having to make appointments, knock on doors and sell himself and his services, the prospect of which was completely overwhelming and totally daunting.

He claims that, given a choice, he would rather have chopped off his right finger than make a sale. Armed with this level of belief, it's not surprising that his first few attempts at selling his services yielded dismal results. He was well beyond his comfort zone and performing badly – not a great combination for creating success.

However, even though he was experiencing massive discomfort, he recognised that he needed to do something radical, otherwise his business was going to fail and fail fast. So he started to take the business of selling seriously, studying those who were already successful. He enrolled for a number of sales-training courses, hating every minute of them, particularly the role-plays. But as he started to use his new-found techniques he found that he started getting different results. He was in control of the sales process more and more, he was asking better questions and started walking out of the door with sales, sometimes more than he went in for!

The tipping point came in his seventh month in business, when he closed more sales in that one month than his previous six months combined. His sales secret?

Sales secret

◆ Understand the consequences of failure. The pain of pushing beyond your boundaries and learning how to sell professionally is far less painful than your business failing.

Now you know how to build your self-belief and regain it quickly when you need to, next you need to understand that to maintain your motivation over the long term, you need to ...

3

Tune into radio station WIIFM

WIIFM RADIO STANDS FOR 'What's in it for me'. When was the last time you tuned in? Highly motivated salespeople have highly motivating goals, so what is it that drives you and keep your juices flowing day after day? If it's not compelling enough, you will lose your motivation and give up when the going gets tough.

It's likely you already have *some* goals; they are usually called 'sales targets'. However, on their own, these are not sufficient to distinguish you as an extraordinary salesperson. These targets need to *mean* something to you personally.

Defining your goals

Clear goals are a secret ingredient in achieving sales success. However, the focus in business is normally placed solely on the monetary value of a person's sales performance. This on its own is not a sufficient driver for you to maintain your long-term motivation, particularly on the tough days.

In today's society we tend to measure success only by how much somebody earns, the size of their house, the type of car they drive, how many people they employ, how much their company stock is worth and so on.

Sales secret

◆ It is unlikely money is your only motivational driver – it's what that money *means* to you that will maintain your focus when the going gets tough.

Financial reward is merely a tool: a vehicle with which to make choices, create something, and most crucially makes you feel something. It's never about the stuff; it's about what the stuff means to you, which is why I always ask people to create goals in more than just monetary terms. This also gives you permission to measure your own success by more than simply your bank balance.

You may have a combination of drivers. Perhaps you would like to live in a modest house, mortgage-free, as that would enable you to feel secure. Maybe you would prefer to work part-time to allow you to spend more time with your family, and you need a certain level of income to maintain your lifestyle yet allow you to reduce your working hours.

Maybe you would like to explore the world and travel, as you are driven by new experiences and a sense of exploration. What about walking on to a plane and turning left, knowing that you can always travel in comfort and style.

Perhaps you want to provide the best education for your children. Or even create a business that provides employment for others. Perhaps you want to leave a legacy, or be known for being the best in your industry, raising customer expectations – and then surpassing them.

Or maybe you want to improve your lifestyle, live in a bigger house in a better location, drive a bigger car, own a bigger telly, dine out in fine restaurants, wear the clothes you want and take better holidays because you draw feelings of joy, comfort and success from these belongings and experiences.

We so often limit our expectations based on what other people would choose for us and how they will judge us if we stretch beyond what *they* deem to be acceptable. However, *your future is your choice* and no one else's, assuming you choose to make those decisions, of course.

It's vital that you clearly define your goals and work out WIIFM. This is not about being selfish, but about being focused. Deciding on what you want is fun, exciting and absolutely your birthright. Remember being a child and writing your Christmas list to Santa Claus before sending it up the chimney? When you were a child you didn't hold back; you asked for what you wanted. Don't be the kind of person who fears making decisions about what you want, for the fear that it won't come true or that others will judge you negatively for your choices.

Sales secret

◆ Link your focus and efforts in your professional life to rewards and goals that motivate you in your *whole* life.

Can anyone guarantee that everything you decide on will absolutely come true? Of course not: that also depends on how you go about it and how hard you work for it. But one thing I absolutely can guarantee is that it definitely won't happen if you don't make that initial choice and decide it's what you *do* want.

First make a list of all of the tangible goals you want to achieve; next record the feeling you most associate with this goal and then decide by when this will be achieved; finally record how much money it will require to make this happen.

Below is a list to help you to start thinking beyond simply 'achieving your sales target'.

◆ Things you may want to acquire

◆ Things you may want to learn

◆ Experiences you may wish to have

◆ Places you'd like to visit

◆ Emotions you would like to feel or feel more of

◆ Relationships you would like to share

◆ Things you would like to create

◆ The difference you want to make to someone or something

The state of mind you are in makes a huge difference as you do this exercise. If you are slouched in a chair, your brain response will be slouched too. You want to engage your creativity and your passion and you need to silence any negative Vicky Pollard voice in your head that may be saying rubbish like 'But that's not possible' or 'How are you doing to achieve that?'

Sales secret

◆ Decide first – the 'hows' will work themselves out later.

Instead, stand up, put on some really upbeat music that makes you feel good. Say your mantra out loud five times (if you haven't thought of one yet, use mine 'All I need is within me now!') and then complete the exercise as outlined below.

My intention is	which makes me feel	by when	I have earned this much to enable me to achieve this goal
to clear my mortgage	very proud, secure and comfortable	1 January 2015	£350,000
own my perfect car	successful and comfortable	23 July 2010	£75,000
pay for my children's education	strong and able to provide for my family	Sept 2012 – July 2044	£120,000
and so on . . .			

I recently completed a coaching session with one of my clients who was reviewing his goal board which we had designed six months earlier which was full of pictures of a fabulous house, a huge office housing his business, a picture of his perfect relationship and he was saying to me 'But it means nothing Nicola, I feel so disconnected from it all'.

I was able to help him reaffirm that the pictures of his goals were nothing to do with the houses or cars, but what the goals represented emotionally for him. So for example, the picture of an Aston Martin represented *'understated success'*, the big office meant *'creating employment and reward for hundreds of people'*, the yacht represented a particular moment in time when he could share his success with his immediate family and friends. Everything was so much more than just the stuff, and once he understood that, he was able to reconnect with his goals and therefore his deeper motivation.

Tuning in every day

Now you have your goals clearly defined, the next step is to programme them into your unconscious mind so that they truly become part of who you are. You need to tune into radio station WIIFM every day. The more your unconscious mind *accepts* your goal as your destiny, the more your behaviour will be focused on a daily basis to create and pursue every opportunity that ensures you fulfil your goals.

Every amazing achievement only ever happened because someone somewhere first made the decision that it would happen. The trick here is to associate your daily achievements at work with something more meaningful for you personally, so that you remain focused even when you're having a tough day, which can turn into a tough week and perhaps even a tough month. So even on the days when you wish you could stay at home, the more compelling your reasons are for getting on with it, the more compelled you are to achieve your goals.

Sales secret

◆ Highly motivated salespeople are first highly disciplined
    salespeople.

There are a number of fun ways in which to tune in daily
to WIIFM. Select a few from the list below and surround
yourself with your own emotional drivers, so that when you
need to, you only have to focus on a goal to remind yourself
why you need to pick yourself up and dust yourself down
and get back out there.

1   Create a visual goal board. Take your list from the
    previous exercise and find pictures that represent your
    goals, preferably with you in them (even if you
    superimpose yourself on to an existing picture), then
    stick the picture to a goal board that you hang
    somewhere where you see it every day. Every time you
    glance at your goals, take a brief moment to focus your
    intentions on *living* that goal and how that feels.

2   Stick a Post-it note to the bathroom mirror, and then
    every morning as you wash your face, you will also
    refocus your mind. Stick a Post-it on a whiteboard in
    your office, or alternatively do as I do and write a goal
    in lipstick across the mirror! No way can you avoid
    them then.

3   Write a cheque to yourself, dated for the day you
    anticipate cashing it and carry it in your wallet or purse.

4   Create a certificate of achievement and frame it.

5   Laminate a goal and place it on the side of your bedside
    cabinet or even on the ceiling above your bed, so that the
    last thing you see at night and the first thing you see in
    the morning is that goal.

6   Create a goal book. Just as you did with the goal board,
    except place your goals within a book that you carry with
    you and flick through every day.

I require everyone that has ever worked in any of my sales
teams to complete this exercise. I obviously want them working hard for me and the business, but their efforts have to
transfer into something meaningful for them. I enjoy seeing
the pictures of them on a luxury holiday with their family, or
driving their dream car, or owning their own home, plastered
all over their desks and I take great joy when they are able to
fulfil those ambitions as a direct result of their own efforts. I
also find as a sales manager that it's extremely useful to know
what motivates the people within my team.

Create short-term rewards

As I've already made clear in this chapter, it is absolutely
crucial that you create a focus for your efforts. However, it
can be pretty soul-destroying if all of your goals are long-
term big goals and it may take you a couple of years to
achieve them; therefore another secret to maintaining your
daily motivation is to create short-term rewards that you can
take great pleasure in achieving.

Making this work requires discipline as, if you always
reward yourself simply because you decide *you're worth it* and

it doesn't relate to any particular effort on your part, then it stops being a reward and instead becomes an indulgence.

Simple rewards can be something as simple as taking a 5-minute break for a cup of tea (it's an English thing!) but only when you reach the end of a particular task, or you've made 20 more sales calls.

Likewise it could be something you purchase that gives you a great feeling of reward as well as remind you of your success. I recently bought myself a very expensive handbag which I use for work, a totally luxury for me and not something I would normally buy. However, I decided to reward myself as a result of winning a particular piece of business. Now everyday as I use that bag I'm reminded of my success and it fuels me on for the next one.

Here are some more examples of short-term rewards that you could use to maintain your motivation and feelings of success.

◆ A new suit or a particular piece of clothing.

◆ A meal in a restaurant, where you order from the menu without looking at the prices, instead choosing the meal and accompanying wine that you want as opposed to making your choices on what you think is good value. (I shall for ever remember a $100 Kobe beef steak I shared during a meal in San Diego in 2005. Absolutely amazing, both the steak and the reason for ordering it!)

◆ The latest CD from your favourite band or singer.

◆ Finishing work an hour early and then using that additional time doing something you enjoy.

◆ Tickets to your favourite sporting or cultural event.

◆ The latest upgrade for your phone, or some other personal gadget.

◆ A luxury weekend away in a hotel of your choice.

Use simple pleasures to reward your efforts regularly, otherwise you could be in danger of losing your motivation if you only feel you will achieve your just desserts when you achieve your bigger goals.

Now tune into WIIFT

Just before we move on from the concept of WIIFM, I want to introduce you to the radio frequency of WIIFT, which stands for 'What's in it for *them*'. Just as you are motivated by much more than monetary gain, your prospects are also driven by a personal set of goals. We have already laid the foundation for understanding that the sales process is much more than a simple sales transaction and involves motivating others into taking action by the transference of your beliefs and emotions on to someone else; your job as a sales professional, as we will discover later, is to relate the client's emotional attachment to your product or service – towards the achievement of your prospect's own personal goals.

So how can buying your product or service help your prospect achieve their own personal goals? When you are able to understand this, you will set yourself far apart from the many mediocre salespeople who only focus on the transactional element of selling.

Now it's time to ...

4

Why some people buy and others fob you off

HAVE YOU EVER WONDERED why some people leap at the opportunity to buy from you while others dither and take ages to reach a decision, and then still come back with a 'Let me think about it'? All of this can be explained by one simple concept – understanding why people buy.

Traditionally we are taught in sales that we must uncover the client's need and match our associated product benefits in order to motivate them to buy from us. This *is* a critical part of becoming a master influencer, but it's not the main reason why people buy from you. Yet even this basic concept is something that even the most experienced salespeople forget: they forget the difference between *features* and *benefits*.

I have a little saying *features tell – benefit sell*. Corny I know, but so true and it helps you to remember the difference between the two. A feature is what something does; the benefit is the difference it makes to the other person. The way I was originally taught the difference between features and benefits about a million years ago is to think of a briefcase and all the features that the briefcase may have, then by asking 'Which means?' to convert those features into benefits. So for example:

It has a handle	**which means**	*it's easier to carry*
There is a secure lock	**which means**	*all your contents will be secure*
It is made of quality leather	**which means**	*it will enhance your image*

And so on . . .

The same principle applies to anything you are hoping to persuade others to agree to; you must think about the benefit in terms of the other person.

What do you really sell?

So what is it you really sell? Does your product solve a problem or a potential problem in some way, therefore removing an emotional headache or making the buyer's life easier in some way? Is it a tangible product: something that the buyer can hold and touch and instantly get a feel for the product's benefits. Or is it a concept sell that will make them feel the benefit only when they've experienced the product for themselves? Ultimately you need to decide how your product or service benefits your customer in some way.

So, for example;

◆ Do you sell mortgages – or are you are selling the sense of pride which comes from owning your own home, or the feeling of providing a safe haven for a family?

- Do you sell greetings cards or gifts – or are you selling the experience of being able to make someone else feel good by giving them a card or a gift?

- Do you sell business services – or are you selling the improvement those services will make to the company's productivity and profitability and how that feels?

- Do you sell a meal in a restaurant – or a dining experience?

- Do you sell holidays – or are you selling the time together with loved ones, the luxury of being looked after by someone else, or even the experience of enjoying a different culture and climate?

- Do you sell clothes – or the experience of wearing those clothes?

- Do you sell books – or knowledge and/or entertainment?

- Do you sell insurance – or a sense of certainty and security?

- Do you sell training – or changes in behaviour?

- Do you sell food – or taste, or convenience, or even health?

- Do you sell gadgets – or a simplified easier lifestyle, or a sense of keeping up with a peer group?

- Do you sell stationery – or the means to communicate more professionally?

I think you get my drift. Take a moment now and draw a line down a piece of paper. On one side of the page list as many of the features that you can think of for your product or service, then on the opposite side document as many benefits as you can muster. You may find that a benefit can be equated to more than one feature – that's fine. Just record as many features and benefits as you can. Remember 'features tell and benefits sell' and keep asking the question 'Which means what?' to reveal the benefits.

Feature	Benefit

I once worked with the telesales department of a holiday company, helping them improve their sales conversions. This was an inbound call centre which took bookings for caravan-park-based holidays. Although the team were known as Telesales Advisers, in my book they were largely Order Takers as the enquiries were 99% inbound and generated largely through the activities of the marketing team. The only true 'sale' they were required to make was to sell the company's own travel insurance as an add-on to the holiday.

When I first arrived, a conversation between a telesales adviser and a customer would often sound similar to this:

Customer: **Can you check the availability for 'X' holiday for the first week in June?**

Adviser: **Yes that's available. I'll book it now, at a cost of £400? Would you like to take our holiday insurance for an additional £18?**

If you were asked that question, what would your natural response be? You would probably have no hesitation in saying 'Er, no thanks'. First, the adviser has no idea what *needs* the client may have, and therefore is unable to present *any relevant benefits* for the insurance package, let alone build an emotional association to the insurance package, where the client feels they *must* have it. It's no wonder their sales conversions were abysmal. Also, owing to the high call volumes, productivity was crucial, so we needed to find a way to get benefits across to the customer simply and quickly without lengthening the call time too much.

When I began work with the telesales team and asked them to complete the exercise to identify the features and benefits of their insurance package, they simply didn't know what they were. Therefore they had no belief in their product. Is it any wonder they hadn't made many sales?

So first we wrote down the longest list of features we could muster for their insurance product. Then we kept asking the 'Which means what?' question until we could find as many benefits as possible. Next we categorised their customers into the three most typical types, which were:

◆ Families with young children

◆ Retired elderly couples

◆ Surfer dudes, holidaying together as a gang of mates.

Each of these three categories of holidaymaker have very different holiday experiences. Young families are more likely to have a minor accident or cause accidental damage to the caravan. Elderly couples are more likely to have health problems needing long-term hospital treatment, and surfer dudes travel with valuable personal items and tend to have the latest mobile phones, MP3 players and cameras which they may leave unsecured as they play in the waves.

Next, we matched the most appropriate benefits to each different type of customer. So, for example, we highlighted the accidental damage benefits to families with young children, the medical care benefits to the elderly couples and the cover for damaged or lost personal items to the surfer dudes. That way, very easily the telesales advisers were able to highlight the most appropriate benefits for each different type of customer.

So now a conversation between an adviser and a customer became one of the following three scenarios.

"From your reservation details I notice that your children are 4 and 6 years old. A fantastic age, but I bet they can be a real handful at times? I wonder if you had considered taking our additional holiday insurance which only increases your holiday cost by £18. That way if you or any of your children fell over and hurt themselves you would have the peace of mind to know that they would receive the best possible treatment. Also if they accidentally caused any damage to your accommodation, which can so easily happen, you wouldn't need to worry, we would take care of any repairs and potential costs to you. We want to make sure that you spend your time on holiday focusing on just that – enjoying your holiday, spending time with your family, not worrying about what might or potentially could happen."

'I wonder if you had considered taking our additional holiday insurance which only increases your holiday cost by £18. I'm sure that you and your wife are in the best of health, but should either of you fall ill whilst on your holiday when you are a long way away from your home, we would ensure you received the best possible hospital treatment and medical care. We would also take care of any additional accommodation or living costs for a family member to stay close by whilst you needed to stay in hospital. Once you were feeling better we would then make sure you got home safely. And in the event that you were unable to go home for some time, we would cover those additional accommodation and living expenses for your family member, for up to 6 months. We want to make sure that you spend your time on holiday focusing on just that – enjoying your holiday, not worrying about what might happen to each other if either of you became poorly.'

'I wonder if you had considered taking our additional holiday insurance which only increases your holiday cost by £18. I assume you will be taking a digital camera, possibly your MP3 player and your mobile phone on holiday with you. Nobody ever likes the thought of losing their personal items or, worse still, having them stolen, which is why most insurance packages only cover them if they are kept on your person or locked in a safe. However, we know that you want to be on holiday out and about enjoying yourself and you may leave your camera in the car, your phone momentarily on a table in a cafe, or even inside your belongings on the beach, and if the worst was to happen – even though it would be inconvenient –

we would ensure that you had your items replaced. That way you can spend your holiday doing just that – enjoying your holiday with your friends, not worrying about where you've left your valuable personal items.'

Now, in a perfect world I would actually recommend that the salesperson goes further, asking more questions, using some of the more advanced techniques that we will learn in Part 2 of this book. But even making these very simple changes and by presenting some *benefits* to the customer, the conversion rate on insurance sales shot up from 11% to 65% and has stabilised between 55% and 60% seven years on.

You gotta make them *feel* something

In the previous section I've alluded to the fact that benefits are not actually the true reasons a potential client will make a purchase: you need to transfer those benefits into something the client desires.

In the first chapter we uncovered a new definition of selling which involves transferring your emotions and beliefs on to your prospect. The final element of understanding why a buyer says 'Yes', is appreciating how those emotions, beliefs and product benefits transfer into the buyer's emotional attachment to the outcomes from making the purchase.

Sales secret

◆ People buy based on emotion then justify their decision with logic.

Your buyer will agree to the sale when they *feel* they will gain something from the delivery of your sales proposition **AND** they *feel* **a perceived sense of loss** if they don't take up the proposition. Simply put, they buy because they have created an emotional attachment to your product or service and feel they can't live without it!

The greater the risk on the buyer's part, the greater the emotional attachment needs to be, which is why we fill our baskets at the supermarket with lower-value items that we buy on the spot just because we've passed them with our trolley. The risk is minimal yet we still believe there is some benefit, which is why we pick them up but without much thought. We take much longer to deliberate upon a higher-value item, as the risk is now much greater. We are thinking 'What if I spend my money and it doesn't fulfil my expectations?'. Once you are convinced you will gain some benefit and the trade-off is worth the risk, you then use any logic to justify your buying decision. **You sell it to yourself!**

Sales secret

◆ A person will take the necessary action and commit to the sale when they associate greater consequences to *not buying*.

A potential buyer is persistently balancing a delicate internal equation: the consequences and proposed outcomes of taking the risk and agreeing to the purchase, against the consequences and potential outcomes if they don't take that risk and agree to the sale.

All of us are motivated by the desire to *move towards pleasure* and pleasant outcomes and the desire to *move away from pain* and outcomes that do not fulfil our expectations. Most people believe they are motivated by their own desires for pleasure and all the rewards that that can bring, whereas psychological findings, and particularly the work of Dr. Alfred Alder, tell us that the human condition is actually more motivated by the desire to avoid pain and negative consequences: obviously physical pain, but also psychological pain – things that do not make us feel good.

So how does this transfer into a sales scenario? These pain/pleasure motivations work in exactly the same way in a buyer's decision-making process: their strongest desire is always to avoid painful consequences. I know potential customers who in our first meeting have outwardly informed me they have no means and no desire to make a purchase, yet later have miraculously found the means necessary because now the thought of not buying the product or service was simply too great. So even though initially they did not perceive a need for my product and had no budget, once they associate emotionally with the outcomes of the sale, they then find a way to take the risk. Once they associate more pain to not buying, it becomes incomprehensible for them not to say 'yes'.

I can't stress this enough. Be under no illusion that your client buys from you simply because you present some snazzy benefits. The benefits simply help them *logically justify their emotional attachment* to the outcomes from the purchase of your product.

So in the previous holiday insurance example, the buyer doesn't make their decision because they like the features and benefits of the medical care, or the accidental damage or even the cover for lost or stolen personal items; they say 'Yes' when the thought of having that extra insurance makes them *feel* something – and in this example it's usually a 'sense of security'. And even then, they will only buy the insurance when the thought of *not feeling* that sense of security is *more painful* than parting with, in this case, £18. In that moment, the customer values that particular emotional connection greater than the pain or risk of parting with the £18 required investment.

Have you ever heard yourself recounting to your family and friends the reasons why you yourself made a recent purchase? You become the best salesperson on the planet when you are justifying your own decisions, especially if you think someone won't approve! Quite frankly, you will spout out any drivel to justify your decision, whereas the real reason you have made the purchase is because the thought of owning that product or benefiting from that service in some way **makes you feel something** and the thought of having to live without it becomes too painful!

For example, have you ever bought a home? Usually you decide what type of features you want your home to have: for example, how many bedrooms and bathrooms; located in what area; what type of garden; is a garage or additional storage important and, most importantly, how much are you prepared (or indeed can afford) to risk in outlaying for your purchase? You then approach your estate agent or search the internet seeking out possible properties that fit your criteria.

Next you embark on the task of viewing some properties and weighing up the pros and cons of each. Some properties on paper will tick all of the boxes, yet step one foot inside and you will know instantly that they are not for you. Other properties, on the other hand, may surprise you and you immediately visualise yourself living in that home, mentally placing your furniture and your personal belongings. Ultimately you will purchase the property that *feels* right, and you wouldn't be the first person if you fell in love with a property that stretches your original budget. But once you've made the emotional attachment to that house, you then use *any* logical means to justify your decision. 'It's on a better street; it has a bigger garden; the kitchen has recently been updated; it has fitted wardrobes; and it's only an extra £20 a month on the mortgage payment' – all of this logical reasoning only serves to cement your decision even more so. The reality is that the prospect of living in that property makes you feel warm and cuddly inside and the thought of *not* living there motivates you even more to take the necessary action to ensure that you have it.

When you are buying a home you usually experience the pain of potential loss whilst you are waiting for the seller to deliberate on your offer. The stronger your emotional attachment to the property, the more your stomach will churn until you've secured the sale and the potential sense of loss is removed.

Yet, many people who sell houses (particularly in the UK) sadly don't understand that they are not selling houses, or even selling homes – they are selling the lifestyle that a particular home can provide. They are selling feelings. So when you make an enquiry, they usually ask you how many bedrooms you want and in what type of area – they only ever enquire about features. Very rarely would it occur to them to ask a question such as 'What type of life do you lead; what does this house need to do in order to make that more enjoyable?'

So think back to your product or service and take your original piece of paper with your list of features and benefits, then add a further column and decide what type of emotions your product can induce in your buyer, as this is what you are *really* selling.

Here are some examples of emotions that drive people to buy.

◆ A sense of security

◆ A feeling of certainty, knowing they are 'right'

◆ A desire for recognition

◆ A feeling of connection, being part of something

◆ A feeling of empathy, giving back or serving in some way

◆ A desire to be more attractive or more loved

◆ To feel proud of an accomplishment

◆ To make someone else feel good

◆ A feeling of fun and enjoyment

◆ A feeling of uncertainty, risk or excitement

◆ To avoid missing out and a feeling of loss

◆ To avoid conflict or a threat of some kind, therefore avoiding feeling fearful

◆ To make their life easier, reducing feelings of stress

◆ Acquiring knowledge or learning something, which can build self-esteem or self-validation

◆ A feeling of health – likewise *not dying* can be a
   massive driver!

This is by no means a complete list, and as you continue
applying the knowledge in this book you will begin to
uncover even more emotional drivers in your buyers.

Even in business-to-business sales, previously you may
have never delved into your customers' reasons for wanting
to purchase your products or services at this deeper emotional level, believing they are only motivated by the desire
to improve productivity, improve profitability, improve quality (particularly if they are government-run or not-for-profit
organisations) and ultimately create more success. You will
improve your sales success no end if you appreciate that
your buyers' motivations, although they may well be hidden,
run a lot deeper. Your job is to uncover them and then associate the benefits of your product to their emotional desires
– the more personal the better.

Sales secret

◆ Even in business-to-business sales a buyer may appear
   to be motivated by moving closer to pleasure, i.e.
   making more money and creating more business
   success, or solving a problem in their business and
   avoiding pain. Their real motivations, however, lie in
   how creating these outcomes really makes them *feel*
   personally. What does business success really *mean* for
   them? Link those outcomes to you, your product and
   your service and they will be unable to say 'No'!

As we continue on our journey to sales success, it's also important to understand how to use this knowledge in a way that guides your buyer. You need to know how to have conversations with purpose and how to use ...

PART 2

Your *sales skills*

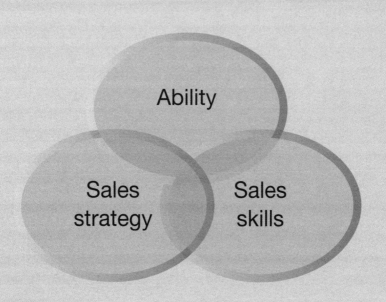

Sales skills

◆ Engage

◆ Qualify

◆ Compel

◆ Commit

◆ Overcome

Part 2 of this book will help you learn and apply the sales *skills* necessary to become super successful. If you have ever wondered why some salespeople just seem to possess those magical sales qualities and ooze 'sales professionalism' from every pore of their body, then the next section will reveal these secret tools that anyone can learn to improve their sales skills. Then in Part 3 we will explore how to apply these skills and develop a sales strategy that works for you.

5

Engage

BEFORE YOU EVEN MEET someone who could become a potential customer (Chapter 10 covers how to go about generating opportunities), you need to be prepared to *engage* them. You need to know how to generate interest in your proposition, how to instantly build rapport with someone and how to create that initial spark of interest, whether you are face to face or engaging them over the telephone.

How many times have you met someone, perhaps at a business event, a social engagement or through an organised business network, and you ask them who they are and what they do. Immediately the other person takes your initial question as an opportunity to verbally 'throw up' all over you! They tell you how great they are, how great their business is and how wonderfully happy all of their customers are. They don't do or say anything that actually engages you; so even though you may be trying to remain focused on them and really listen to what they're saying, it's inevitable that you lose interest and your mind wanders and your eyes glaze over. They've failed to spark any interest from you and the only motivation they've placed in you is the desire to move away as fast as possible from such a bore!

Sales secret

◆ Interesting people are those that appear most *interested*. Ask intelligent questions that get the prospect thinking. Ask questions that invite the prospect to share even more information about themselves.

What about in a retail scenario, if someone happens to be browsing through some items in a store and a retail assistant approaches them and asks if they need any help? More often than not the customer will respond with a pre-rehearsed 'No thank you, I'm just looking'. Sometimes, they actually do want help, but because the sales assistant has failed to engage the customer, the customer simply brushes them off. Even in a telesales scenario, unless you find creative ways to engage the other person, expect a very short and simple fob-off.

Design a Punchy Prologue

The way you introduce yourself is very important. You want to leave your prospect wanting more, open to listening to you and curious about you and your product. Ironically, the way to do this is to hold back as this is a time when less is more, so rather than drivel on with a monotonous over-rehearsed introduction of boring facts and features, you need to deliver a 'punchy prologue'.

Think of a good trailer for a film. A trailer is different from an advert which is designed to explain some benefits and include a 'call to action', usually to make a purchase or take action in some way; whereas a trailer acts as a prologue to the full-length film. It includes some snippets of the content but in a way that builds the anticipation without revealing the entire plot, thus leaving you hungry to find out more. It engages you, and that is the purpose your punchy prologue should fulfil.

Whenever you are in a situation and someone asks you 'What is it you do?', what do you normally say? Have you ever put much thought into your reply? If not, you could be in danger of falling into the trap explained earlier.

Following a keynote speech I gave recently at a national conference, I spent some time browsing round the exhibition hall talking to some of the companies who were exhibiting at the conference. The conference was focused on Leadership and People Development so most of the companies at the exhibition were offering training and consultancy services of some kind. However, I was amazed at the overall poor standard of introductions from the salespeople in the exhibition. Almost all sounded virtually the same. None captured my imagination or made me want to give them any information about me or my company, let alone ask any more questions of them.

Most people's introductions were along the lines of:

'We are a unique training company based in London; we offer training and consultancy in Leadership, Management and Personal Development. We have worked successfully with blue-chip organisations, public sector as well as some smaller companies. We offer a wide range of services designed to fulfil any need you may have.'

Well, so what? At no point did any of these salespeople say anything distinctive or different to me, or found a way to engage my interest further. My usual response was to smile politely and walk away quietly (but writing down the name of the company to contact them later as a potential lead in dire need of my services!).

So what could you say to your prospects? A punchy prologue that gives a short explanation of what you do, yet leaves the client wanting more?

Sales secret

◆ Your prospect will be forming an opinion of you within the first few seconds of meeting you. Stand out from the pack. What you say as a way of introduction will set the tone for any ongoing relationship. If what you say is ordinary, they will assume you, your company and your product is ordinary. Say something inspiring, different and emotionally engaging – and that is what they will assume about your proposition.

A punchy prologue should fulfil the following criteria: be 10 seconds or less; engaging; distinctive; and naturally invite the question 'So how do you do that?'.

1 **Be 10 seconds or less** – any longer and your prospect will start to lose interest. Ideally you want to get your prologue across in one sentence. Remember interesting people are those who are most *interested*. Everyone prefers to talk about themselves; therefore you will not

generate much interest by talking *to* your prospect. Instead you want to spark their interest so that they will want to ask you questions which opens up the opportunity to start a conversation.

2   **Be engaging** – remember, your prospect will be picking up on your beliefs and emotions, so your prologue needs to be delivered with passion and enthusiasm. This is your client's first glimpse of your levels of belief and if you don't feel it, they won't either. So make your prologue personal and speak from your heart. I do believe scripts have their purpose when you are learning a new technique, but once you have mastered the words, throw any scripts away and speak naturally. How would you speak to someone you had known for some time? People respond openly and warmly when you are personable, open and warm towards them.

3   **Be distinctive** – stand out from the crowd. Think of the most creative way of introducing your company to a prospect, even if it may appear a bit wacky or off the wall. People will remember you. Think back to the real reasons why someone buys from you. How can you build some of those elements into your introduction?

4   **Naturally invite the question 'So how do you do that?'** – if your client is left wanting to know more about what you do, then you've successfully created that spark of interest. You've left them with an unanswered question which their curiosity will want answered. By inviting a question from them, it leaves you open to ask more questions in return and a conversation will ensue.

I normally respond to a request for more information from the other person with a probing question such as 'Do you mind if I ask you a couple of questions too?' and before you know it, you now have control of the conversation and are able to move them on to the next stage of the process – qualification.

Here are some real-life examples of punchy prologues. See if from these initial introductions you can work out the product or service on offer.

◆ We facilitate communication.

◆ I'm an electrician – a body electrician.

◆ We help people keep more of their money.

◆ We relight the fire in the belly of your salespeople.

◆ We add life to days, when days can't be added to life.

◆ We turn your house into somewhere you can call your home.

◆ In an ever increasingly crowded marketplace we ensure you are seen by more potential customers.

◆ We create special memories.

◆ We stop you wanting to throw your computer out of the window when it won't work properly.

◆ We build long-term health in your body.

Did you guess correctly? Were you left intrigued, wanting to know more? Below is an explanation of each company together with an example of their previous poor introductions that definitely didn't inspire or engage.

A company offering office stationery

Old prologue	We provide all your stationery needs at the most competitive prices around.
New prologue	We facilitate communication.

A reflexologist

Old prologue	I'm a reflexologist.
New prologue	I'm an electrician – a body electrician!

An accountant

Old prologue	We can fulfil all of your accounting needs.
New prologue	We help you keep more of your money.

Aurora Training (Yes, this is one that my sales team and I use.)

Old prologue	We're a training and coaching consultancy that specialises in Sales, Leadership and Personal Development (I'm almost falling asleep just writing this drivel!)
New prologue	We put the FIRE back in the belly of your sales team.

An end-of-life hospice

Old prologue	We're a hospice.
New prologue	We put life into days when days can't be added to life.

A furniture store

Old prologue	We sell furniture.
New prologue	We turn your house into somewhere you can call home.

A search engine optimisation company

Old prologue	We provide search engine optimisation.
New prologue	In an ever increasingly crowded marketplace we ensure you are seen by more potential customers.

A photographer

Old prologue	I'm a photographer.
New prologue	We create special memories.

A company offering technical business support

Old prologue	We provide technical support.
New prologue	We stop you wanting to throw your computer out of the window when it won't work properly.

An osteopath

Old prologue	I run an osteopath clinic.
New prologue	We help to build long-term health in your body.

Now they are engaged, keep them engaged

OK so now you've got their attention, and they've likely asked the question 'How do you do that?' You need to have a further response at the ready. This next statement needs to accomplish two objectives:

1 Include a sexy benefit that will *hook* them even further:

2 Open a continued dialogue that allows you to move forward on to the qualification stage in the sales process.

Take a moment to look back at your features and benefits that you listed earlier and decide how you could include a benefit to the customer in your response, following a request for more information.

Here are a few more examples for the companies above. Again, see if you can work out which statement matches which company.

> *'We provide on-site and home support hospice care for people and their families who are living with a life-limiting illness, in a way that enables them to feel empowered, prepared for their uncertain future and provides an environment that allows them to enjoy the time they have remaining. However, I'm interested to know what is it you do?'*

> *'We provide osteopathic care for acute problems and also on an on-going basis by working with your body to achieve your optimum alignment which enables your system to build a strong immune system and improve your overall health. Just like a regular check-up at the dentist, we work to protect your spine against long-term erosion, ensuring you stay pain-free and healthy for as long as possible. Can I ask, have you ever visited an osteopath or chiropractor?'*

> *'We supply high-quality, great-value office products on a same-day or next-day replenishment basis, so if you've forgotten to order a printer toner and you have an urgent document to print, we take the stress out of that situation. Tell me, what does your company do?'*

*'We are a long established firm of accountants with years of experience of working with businesses. We obviously like to count the numbers but we want to **affect** the numbers, ensuring you are maximising your full business potential and then working with you to support your ongoing wealth-generation plans. Let me ask, if you were to roll forward 10 years, what would be your ultimate financial goal?'*

'We offer coaching, training and consultancy to companies that have a desire to improve profits and improve their sales revenue. Let me ask you if there was one thing you could change in your business right now what would that be?'

At no point have any of the salespeople mentioned their company name, their fantastic track record, their amazingly happy customers, or how brilliant they are. At this point the prospect is still forming their initial opinion of you as well as the company. They are not interested in anything other than themselves, and blowing smoke up your own chimney only turns them off, which is why to keep them engaged you need to plant a seed in their mind that *they* could potentially benefit in some way. This way they are much more likely to be open with you once you start to ask more probing questions.

In fact, if they are a salesperson themselves they are probably weighing you up as a prospect for *their* company and you need to initially overcome that desire in their mind to immediately sell to you – by hooking them onto the potential benefits for them and their organisation. This way you have much more control of the conversation moving forward.

Gaining appointments over the telephone

The above examples are easy to implement when you are face to face with your prospect: however, how do you engage someone if they are not expecting your call? First, let me be clear about some of my personal opinions with regards to making cold contact with a prospect via the telephone. I always recommend face-to-face contact wherever possible, particularly if you are selling business to business, or in the service industries. I remember the introduction of the fax machine, followed by the internet and videoconferencing: initially, some 'doom and gloomers' predicated that these improvements in technology would kill the need to meet up personally. Yet even with the technological advances in recent history, we still prefer to conduct business or deliver an outstanding customer experience through face-to-face contact. So unless your business model is based on lots of consumer transactions that require no personal contact at all (for example, a pure internet business), always aim to have a coffee with your prospect and 'press the flesh' – it always means much more.

When I first started my business I had no existing client base to work with so I needed to meet people and meet them fast. So for the first 18 months of trading I adopted Jeffrey Gitomer's (the author of *The Sales Bible* and *The Little Red Book of Selling*) '50 bum rule', which basically means if there was an event with 50 butts in the room, my booty was in there too! I accepted every invitation; I went to every networking event, every awards dinner and even to the opening of an envelope. I'm only kidding with the last one, but that is what it felt like.

My intention was to meet as many people as possible, which I would then follow up with a phone call to gain an appointment. This way at least they had heard my Punchy Prologue face-to-face and I had probably started to qualify them at that initial meeting.

The next best way to make contact via the telephone is on the back of a referral. That way you are simply following someone else's instructions to call the prospect and if they respect the other person, they are much more likely to listen to you, for a few moments at least, usually enough to get them engaged.

However, if there is absolutely no way you can avoid making initial contact with a prospect except via the telephone, then decide to enjoy it! Accept that it is high risk and that your hit rate will be lower than if you were being introduced face-to-face; however, if you are upbeat, positive and still embrace the guidelines outlined for developing your punchy prologue, you *will* have success. What's the worst-case scenario? They shout at you, or put the phone down – then great, they're not wasting any more of your valuable time! Move on and make the next call – quick!

However, appreciate that a cold call is always:

◆   an interruption and therefore probably inconvenient;

◆   a situation where the customer is not expecting to be sold to, and is likely to be resistant to any hints that this is a sales call;

◆   a scenario where the customer has no concept of what you may be able to do for them;

◆ only an opportunity to sell the next stage in the sales
process – which is likely to be an initial exploratory
meeting, not to close the end sale.

Therefore, embrace all of this. Remember that all the time
any buyer is equating the pain/pleasure spectrum in their
mind. They will be equating the *pain* of dealing with this
interruption and giving up their time on the phone, to the
pain of missing out of what you have to say. In a telesales
call, even more so than face to face, you need to overcome
these initial hurdles just to engage the client to want to
listen to you. My strategy is to disarm them by
acknowledging these inconveniences up front and get them
on the table straight away. So, for example:

> *'Good afternoon Mr. Smith I know you are not expecting
> my call and I know how inconvenient it can be to be
> interrupted, so I'll keep this brief. The reason I'm calling is
> that I've researched your company/your name has been
> mentioned to me recently by 'X' and I/they believe you may
> benefit from some of the services we offer. We work with
> organisations that have a desire to improve their profits
> and sales performance by relighting the FIRE in the belly of
> your sales team; however, other than my initial research, I
> know very little about your organisation, your goals, the
> current challenges you face or your plans for the future and
> would therefore welcome the opportunity to open a dialogue
> between our organisations. Do you mind if I ask you a
> couple of quick questions. If you could change one thing in
> your organisation right now, what would that be?'*

Sales secret

◆ Don't ask a question until you've stated a benefit that
   will act as a hook in the conversation.

Getting past a gatekeeper

Gatekeepers can be fierce: very often part of their job is to
keep salespeople at bay and avoid any unsolicited interrup-
tions to their boss. Once again follow the procedure above,
only this time accept that you are now selling the opportunity to speak to the buyer. Before you use the example script
below, simply assume that you will be put through and ask
to speak to them. If they block your enquiry then you will
need to give them more benefits.

> *'Good afternoon. Could you put me through to*
> *David Smith?'*

(Note: Always use both their fore and surname as opposed
to Mr or Mrs. It makes your call appear more personal and
they are more likely to assume you already have an existing
relationship with the buyer.)

   If they block your request then follow up with:

> *'I know he's not expecting my call but I have no intention*
> *of wasting his time. The reason I'm calling is that I've*
> *researched your company/David's name has been mentioned*
> *to me recently by 'X' and I/they believe he may benefit from*
> *a quick chat. I'll keep it brief, and if I'm on the phone more*
> *than 1 minute it's because he wants me to be.'*

Depending on their next question, here are some further example responses.

What is it regarding?

'**We work with organisations helping them improve their profits and sales performance by relighting the FIRE in the belly of your sales team; however, other than my initial research, I know very little about your organisation, the company goals, the current challenges or the plans for the future. I only wish to ask a couple of quick questions to see if what we do is appropriate for your organisation. I promise I have no desire to waste any of his time or indeed my own if there is no benefit to continuing a conversation.'**

They're in a meeting; can I take your number and ask them to call you back?

'**No problem – when would be a good time to call back?'**

(Note: They'll NEVER call you back, and if you use this approach instead, the next time you call, you simply ask to be put through as *they've asked you to call!*)

Can you send me some information and I'll pass it on to them?

'**Of course – however, I would need to ask a couple of very quick questions to work out which would be the most relevant information to send, so can you pop me through now so that I can clarify what to send?'**

(Note: Never send information without speaking to the buyer, it will be filed straight in the bin and is a waste of your marketing material, your time in stuffing the envelope and a wasted walk to the post office! As an absolute last resort, direct them to your website whilst arranging an appropriate time to call back.)

Finally, make sure you persist – very often gatekeepers will relent over time – and make sure you do call back at the time you've agreed.

Here are some final dos and don'ts when making appointments via the telephone.

Do:

◆ Ensure you sound as if this is the first and only phone call you are making today – every time.

◆ Do your research. Read the press, Google the company details, ring up the purchasing department and pretend to be a prospect so that you can learn more about the organisation, all before you make your sales call.

◆ Ask for the buyer by name. Find out beforehand, even if it means making a pre-call to the sales call. Starting a sales call by asking 'Who is the most appropriate person to speak to regarding' and then asking to be put through to that person instantly demonstrates that the call is not personal, probably not the first call you've made that day, and is a red flag to a gatekeeper to hold you at bay.

◆ Stand up if you need to get more energy moving in your body.

◆ Focus on your goal board to keep you motivated in a long session of telesales calls.

- Give yourself short rewards, i.e. I'll go for lunch when I've made five more appointments.

- Make friends with the gatekeeper as opposed to perceiving them as hostile: they often have more influence than you may be aware of and they can be a great source of information.

- Ask to speak to their own sales team, for all the inside gossip that could be useful when making your case, i.e. *'I was thinking of contacting David Smith with regards to opening a dialogue, and I wondered if there was any information you may be able to share that would help me in gaining an appointment. Do you mind if I ask a few quick questions? What is the biggest frustration in your role right now?'*

- Take telesales calls in your business: they are often a great source of sales leads i.e. *'Before I answer your questions, do you mind if I ask a couple of my own? Who would be the best person to speak to regarding your sales training?'* Call back when you say you will. Keep persisting – follow up, follow up, follow up.

Don't:

- *Expect them to call you back – they won't.*

- Leave your message on an answer machine. Instead, make sure you diary a further follow-up call.

- Expect them to remember you when you do call back.

- Send any information by post.

- Make an initial contact via email, which has even less personality than a telesales call!

- Make the call unless you are in a 'peak state'. Take a break, go for a short walk or drink some water if you need to reinvigorate your energy levels.

- Take any rejection personally.

- Get angry.

- Allow them to put you on hold unless absolutely necessary: instead, agree a time to call back.

- Be taken for a mug. If the gatekeeper says the buyer is not in the office, but you can hear the person in the background shouting 'Tell them I'm not in' politely call them on it. *'I'm surprised you've said that as I can hear them clearly in the background. If now is not a convenient time for them to speak, perhaps it would be better if I called them back later – when would be a more convenient time for them to come to the phone?'*

Try a few approaches; change what doesn't work; take note of your successes and ultimately find out what works for you, your style, your business and your industry. However, what is absolutely guaranteed to deliver no results is if you don't take any action at all and fail to engage anybody in the first instance! So make a commitment now and decide how many appointments you need in a week or over the month, and if you are not generating enough via other means then book the time in your diary and start hammering the phones.

Next we are going to look at the ways in which, now you have them hooked, you can build rapport with your prospect.

We like people who are like us

We are naturally drawn to people who are like us: people who are similar in age, have similar interests, share similar beliefs or similar life experiences. Therefore, it is also true that if we need to make someone feel more comfortable with us, we need to become more like them. This 'likeness' is what creates the feelings of rapport.

Most people would describe 'rapport' as feeling comfortable with someone. Conversation flows more easily when you are in rapport with someone and they are much more likely to trust what you say: therefore building rapport makes the sales process much easier.

Sales secret

◆ Successful selling, although measured by how many 'transactions' you make, is only possible once you have built a 'relationship' with your customer. Focus on building relationships and the transactions will follow.

The amazing thing about creating rapport is that it is possible to build rapport naturally and easily with absolutely anybody, no matter whom they are or what context you meet them in. It is a skill you already know how to use, as you already build rapport naturally with the people you like!

Wouldn't it be fantastic if you only ever had to engage with people with whom you shared natural rapport, so you only had to sell to people you liked! Obviously that's never going to be the case, which is why it's important to know *how* to build rapport when you need to make the other person feel at ease. Selling under rapport doesn't feel pressured or uncomfortable: instead the prospect will feel like they are hanging out with someone they like and someone who wants to listen to them, someone who has their best interests at heart and who wants to help them – which obviously you do.

Sales secret

◆ Until you qualify the opportunity, assume everyone could be a potential customer and build rapport with everyone.

How to build rapport

Building rapport doesn't mean that you change your values, beliefs or your hairstyle! It simply means you need to find some commonalities between you and the customer that you can use and highlight, that will make the other person feel at ease.

Matching and mirroring

The simplest method of doing this is known as 'matching and mirroring' and involves reflecting back the other person's subtle rapport signals that they generate in the initial stages of the conversation. Remember, this is something that you already do when you naturally feel comfortable with someone: all you are doing here is re-learning how to actively apply this when that natural rapport doesn't already exist either because you don't know the other person, or you find yourself in a situation that feels tense and uncomfortable.

Here are some examples of the signals that someone may use that you can reflect back to them.

Voice qualities: This is one you probably won't need to try too hard to master, as it's normal to naturally match and mirror someone's voice, without much conscious effort. If you meet someone who talks very quietly and you are a naturally loud person, it's likely you would adjust your volume to match that of the person you are talking to. The same philosophy applies to pace, pitch and tone. Don't, however, attempt to mirror a strong regional dialect or accent as this may come across as patronising and false. Speak in your normal dialect but just adjust your other voice qualities.

Phrases: What we say is a direct reflection of what we think. Therefore, if you want to build a connection with someone, it's crucial to use *their* language. That means you need to listen to what they say and the words they use, then slot them back into your conversation when your summarise or ask them more detailed questions. It makes them feel as if you *really* understand their issue or concerns.

When I'm working with a client and I ask a defining question and then record their answers, I'm very observant and ensure I only use their language and not my interpretations of their language. So, for example, if someone says 'I struggle making sales calls', I make a mental note of their exact phrase, even if in my head I could interpret the same phrase as 'I find sales calls difficult'. Although you may think these two phrases mean the same thing, they don't to the person that said 'I struggle making sales calls'.

The next time you have a conversation with someone, *really* listen to the phrases they use as their words have more emotional meaning to them than any variation you may interpret.

> *Sales secret*
>
> ◆ Make notes as you listen to the client. Write down key words and phrases then mark them off as you reflect them back in your conversation. That way you will be sure you have matched and mirrored their phrases.

I use mind maps to make my notes. It's a brilliant way to record a lot of information very quickly. If a client uses a phrase more than once, say, for example 'develop talent', I will underline or circle that phrase in my notes as I recognise that as a key phrase. When I come to explain my proposition I make sure I explain how I will 'develop talent' within their organisation.

Body shape: Whether you're sitting or standing together, pay attention to the other person's stance and then mirror them. Are their hands in or out of their pockets? Do they stand on one leg or are they centred? What is the angle of their shoulders and head?

If you are sitting down, do they have their legs crossed or uncrossed? How do they have their hands placed? Are they leaning forward or relaxed back in their chair. Mirror their body shape exactly and you will build rapport quickly and easily.

Gestures: Very often people have gestures they develop that are particular to them. When they speak, how do they emphasise a point? Do they clasp their hands together, or place one hand out in front? Pay attention to any specific gestures, then use them in your conversation.

I remember once working with someone who used his right index finger to simultaneously tap the end of the fingers on his left hand as he was speaking. I mirrored this and I swear I thought his eyes were going to pop out of his head, as unconsciously he seemed to be thinking 'Wow, she's a finger tapper just like me'.

Handshake: In the business world the normal form of greeting in a business context is to extend your right hand and offer someone a handshake. This is often the first physical contact you make with your prospect, and an untold amount of communication can be made via this one gesture. Generally speaking, people will judge each other based on the strength they feel in a person's handshake: so if someone greets you with a limp handshake, you form an opinion that they are weak; likewise a strong firm handshake gives the impression of strength and confidence.

As a general rule of thumb, match the intensity of the other person's handshake. If they clasp their hand over the back of yours into a two-handed handshake, mirror them and clasp your left hand on the back of theirs. If they use their left hand to touch your arm, elbow or even shoulder, mirror them back. Even though this may appear bold, it helps to build a stronger connection.

Dress code: There are four main types of business dress; Black Tie, Lounge Suit, Business Attire and Smart Casual.

For a man these are usually pretty straightforward to comply with, whereas a woman's interpretation can be less obvious. Black Tie can mean a long formal evening gown, or a shorter cocktail dress. Lounge Suit usually refers to a cocktail dress. Business Attire can mean a smart outfit generally with a jacket, and whereas Smart Casual can simply mean the removal of a man's tie and the unbuttoning of his top button, it can be open to vast interpretation by women. In the creative industries you may even be tempted to include a further dress code called 'Funky', which can mean almost anything goes – pink hair, body piercings, the works!

Ideally to build rapport you want to mirror your prospect's dress code, which means you may have to include this as part of your research. Are they a 'funky' organisation that would not warm to someone who walks in wearing a pin-stripe suit, or do they dress more formally and are less likely to take you seriously if you turn up in jeans and a jacket. I recommend wearing clothes that make you feel comfortable, boost your confidence and display the image you want to portray. If unsure, I prefer to be over-dressed than under-dressed, and in my case 'Funky' doesn't even enter my dress vocabulary so I don't even attempt it! Although I very rarely wear a full pin-striped business suit in my day-to-day work, preferring instead smart jeans and a jacket, I would dress super smart for a first meeting with a new prospect if I was unsure.

Sales secret

◆ Dress for the job you want, not necessarily the job you have.

Interests: Before you meet your prospect, particularly if you are meeting them on their premises, you want to find some common interests which you can use to initiate a conversation. Remember interesting people are those who are most interested. Do they enjoy a particular sport, holiday destination; do they have a family or have they won an award recently? Look for clues as you walk into their environment, or ask these questions when you do your research. You can even use this as an opportunity to build rapport with the gatekeeper, e.g. 'Tell me, does David Smith have a sport he particularly enjoys?'

If matching and mirroring is completely new to you, then you might be feeling a bit concerned, even worried that you'll end up looking silly in your attempts to mirror the other person, or that there's something a bit false about copying people's body language. Remember this is something that you already do unconsciously when you feel comfortable with someone.

Trust me, try it out and you will see how easy it is to create rapport.

Sales secret

◆ Make small adjustments and mirror as you naturally talk to the other person: that way it won't feel as if you are copying them. Being relaxed is the key.

Pace and Lead

You know you have achieved strong rapport when the other person starts to copy you! This is what is known as Pace and

Lead and happens when someone feels an affinity with you. They do say imitation is the highest form of flattery.

Watch out for Pace and Lead as a signal for how much rapport you've created. Try purposely changing your body stance and see if the other person copies you. If so, you can feel confident that they feel an empathy with you. In a sales meeting, cross or uncross your legs to check how much rapport exists. If there is still a resistance, then keep reflecting their mannerisms until that natural state of rapport is created.

Identifying Pace and Lead is also the way to work out who is the rapport leader in a group scenario. Watch the body language of the other people and see whose body language they're copying. One of my clients is a Japanese manufacturing firm and there is one Japanese manager who has quite a distinctive gesture of twiddling his pen. In team meetings, if someone else wants to get the attention of the group just before making a point, you can observe them start to twiddle their pen in exactly the same way. Before you know it all 12 team members are simultaneously twiddling pens, wanting to hold the control of the group rapport.

If you find yourself in this type of situation, perhaps when you are making a sales presentation to a panel, mirror the rapport leader first, then you will automatically be able to lead the other members of the group.

Now you have engaged your prospect and made them feel comfortable by building rapport. Next it's important to …

6

Qualify

IT'S IMPORTANT TO ENSURE a true opportunity exists between you and the prospect. Attempting to 'sell' when the only guaranteed outcome is rejection is a fool's game. Making sure you qualify your prospect seems so obvious but I'm always surprised just how many people fail to establish the client's circumstances, which leaves them unable to tailor their sales presentation. Instead they are drawn to anybody and everybody who shows an interest no matter how small, or they believe that if they keep on selling, at some point something they say will be relevant.

Qualification is a key part and I would personally say *the most important* sales skill to master. Fully understanding your prospect's circumstances allows you to guide the conversation in the direction that will lead to a sale. It allows you to omit information from your presentation that would not be relevant and enables you to gain the most appropriate commitment from every sales interaction, even if that does not mean a closed sale but, perhaps, an escalation to the Ultimate Decision Maker or gaining some referrals from the contact.

Therefore, you need to know how to ask the most appropriate questions which guide the buyer through the qualification process. In this chapter we will look briefly at the different types of questioning and a structure which I call 'The Hot Button' which will guide your questioning.

Sales secret

◆ Develop interesting questions that really make your client think. Asking the same old questions that every other salesperson asks will only illicit well-rehearsed responses from your client. Ask questions that make them think.

Choosing the right question

There are four main types of questions that you can use with your client. Each have their place and each can either help or hinder you as you proceed in the conversation. The main skill in questioning is knowing what to ask and when to ask it, before carefully listening to the response and tailoring your next question accordingly. That's why we have two ears and one mouth!

Sales secret

◆ Rather than 'interrogate' your client with a long list of questions, build them into a conversation, making sure to remember the relevant pieces of information that are revealed from their responses.

Varying the types of questions you ask avoids the discussion feeling more like a grilling and helps to build up two-way communication. Also the different types of questions can be useful at different points in the conversation.

Open questions

An open question is one that cannot be answered with a simple positive or negative response; the prospect must supply an *explanation*. It is difficult to respond to an open question with a one-word answer.

They are great at opening a dialogue and gaining a more descriptive response. They are particularly useful at the beginning of the conversation when you need to invite the customer to engage in a conversation.

Here are some examples of open questions:

◆ *What made you decide to relocate your business to this part of the world?*

◆ *What has been the biggest challenge to your organisation over the past 18 months?*

◆ *What would need to happen now in order to move ahead?*

◆ *Is there a reason you've not tackled this problem before now?*

◆ *How will you know when you have received value for money?*

Closed questions

Unlike open questions, closed questions require a definitive response, usually a 'Yes' or a 'No'. They are useful to clarify a person's opinion or how they feel. They are great when you need to confirm facts, clarify understanding or to summarise your understanding of their opinions.

For example:

◆ *Does that feel like a suitable solution for you?*

◆ *If we get the deal right, can we have the business?*

◆ *Am I correct in understanding that what you've outlined so far is ...?*

Probing questions

Probing questions are ideally used as a follow-up to an open question, allowing you to dig for more specific information. Also, you can use a probing question to stimulate the buyer's thinking or plant a seed in their mind which you can then link back to your product benefits.

For example:

◆ *That's interesting. What specifically made you choose that course of action?*

◆ *What precisely would be an acceptable timescale for delivery?*

◆ *Why is that so important?*

(You can also create a probing question by simply repeating their previous statement 'I enjoy networking'.)

◆ *Really, tell me why do you enjoy networking?*

Multiple questions

When used correctly multiple questions can be very powerful. They allow you to create choices. They are particularly useful when you want to gain a commitment out of the prospect as both options can result in committing to an action; you are simply asking them to choose which option they would prefer.

- *When would be the best time to meet up – Tuesday morning or Wednesday afternoon?*

- *Would you prefer all items delivered together or each item dispatched as they become available?*

- *Which is more important – travelling by the most cost-effective method, or travelling in comfort?*

A word of warning, however: avoid using multiple questions at the beginning of a conversation, as too many options will confuse the customer and instead they will answer with the information *they* want to tell you. Instead focus on open and probing questions when you are drawing information out of them.

Now you know how to ask questions let's put them into a simple format that allows you to professionally qualify the opportunity.

Uncover their Hot Button

As a guideline, you should be spending 80% of your time engaging your client, building rapport and qualifying the opportunity. Only 20% of the sales conversation should be you presenting your opportunity and gaining the client's commitment. Spend more time doing the legwork up front and the rest becomes really easy.

The Hot Button **is** the key to the sale. By following this format you will uncover your buyer's motivations for the sale, their concerns, their buying power and any potential blocks that could stop the sale progressing.

Sales secret

◆ You will negate almost all potential objections that could appear later by clarifying information up front.

The Hot Button is a brilliant structure to follow as it acts as a mental tick box to ensure you've gathered all the information you need before moving forward and compelling the client to make a commitment.

The Hot Button is made up of five parts:

◆ Their wants

◆ Their needs

◆ Their wounds

◆ Their authority

◆ Their resources.

Their wants and needs

So what are wants and needs and what is the difference between the two? Depending on your business model and how you engage your clients, their wants may be fairly obvious. If a person walks into a car showroom, it's a given that they are at least thinking about *wanting* a car. The salesman's job is simply then to clarify what type of car and model they really want.

If you receive a phone call from a potential client or you generate sales leads for your business either from referrals or as a result of other forms of marketing, then you can assume that the client wants something you offer. If, however, you are meeting a new prospect for the first time or you are making a cold contact, you will need to uncover, perhaps even plant in their mind, what they may want. In this scenario a simple open question will uncover their basic wants.

- *What is it you desire?*
- *If there was one thing you could change in your business right now what would that be?*
- *What is your biggest frustration?*
- *What was the reason that made you contact our organisation?*
- *Are you aware of who we are and what we offer?*

(In case you hadn't spotted, the last option on the list is actually a closed question. If they answer 'Yes' then follow it with one of the previous examples; if they answer 'No' then it leads nicely into your punchy prologue.)

However, what clients *want* and what they *need* are very different. Until you drill down and understand what a client needs you are unable to present a compelling sales proposition.

A client's need is a much stronger pull, as it is their emotional attachment to the outcome. Remember, people make their decision based on what they expect to feel as a result of the transaction, and their need is what they *need to feel*. It's the intangible element of the sale.

> *Sales secret*
>
> ◆ Be careful not to confuse wants and needs. A client may
> sometimes describe what they want but use the
> language of 'I need'. For example, 'I need a new washing
> machine because mine has broken'. In this instance
> although they are describing *needing* a new washing
> machine, in fact this is actually what they want. How
> they expect to feel when they have purchased a new
> washing machine is their need. The expectation of this
> *feeling* is their emotional attachment, or what I describe
> as a need, to the outcome and the driving force behind
> their buying decision.

So no matter what a client has told you about what they
want – 'I need a new car', 'I want more sales', 'I must have a
holiday' – your goal now is to uncover an emotional *need* in
your client that your product can potentially fulfil.

For example, if they have a need to feel safe and you offer
insurance, then that's an obvious match. However, unless
you ask the right questions you may never uncover their true
need, especially if they are disguising it with *wants.*

The easiest way to delve deeper into needs is to respond
to a client's initial responses with more probing questions:

◆ *Why is that so important?*

◆ *What does that really mean to you?*

◆ *How will you know when we have achieved your desired outcomes?*

Then keep repeating this type of question until they start to
reveal some emotional attachments to their desired outcomes.

Once you get your head around this, you really will set yourself apart from most salespeople. Recently I worked with a group of retailers who, owing to the credit crunch and the current economic downturn, are all finding business pretty tough. In the group we had representatives from a wide variety of companies all selling different types of products: John Lewis department store, Clinton Cards who sell cards and gifts, Fraser Hart a jewellers, Past Times a unique gift store, Jack Jones a man's clothing store and Specsavers who sell glasses and eyewear. Initially, although everyone understood the concept that consumers buy based on emotion and justify with logic, transferring that theory to uncovering their customers' needs proved to be a bit of a leap. However, by the end of the session everyone was able to appreciate some of the potential driving emotional needs their customers may have.

◆ People give cards because it makes them feel good to know that by giving a card it makes the other person feel good.

◆ People buy clothes to portray a certain image, which makes them feel confident.

◆ People buy glasses and designer frames, again, not just for the quality but because they want to own a designer-name pair of frames and in doing so it makes them feel good about themselves.

◆ People buy jewellery either as a gift or for themselves for exactly the same reasons.

You must, must, must uncover these emotional reasons for buying if you are going to sell your products professionally.

This also applies in business sales, even though you may not naturally assume the buyer has any *personal* emotional attachment to the buying decision – they do! Do not be fooled by assuming that they are only driven by the cheapest option or want the best deal. Let me share an example of a real-life scenario in the business-to-business environment.

I attended a meeting recently with an existing customer who had asked me to discuss the possibility of running a 'motivational' training session with some of their staff, following a recent restructure. Now, even though this was a warm enquiry from a client that we had worked with previously, I still needed to qualify this opportunity.

Just to contextualise the conversation below, the client is a pharmaceutical wholesaler and retailer who had recently purchased a regional independent chain of pharmacy stores, doubling the size of their retail business overnight. This massive change had instantly thrown the business into chaos, creating a huge amount of operational challenges within the organisation – hence the reason for the enquiry.

Here is a summary of our discussion.

> Nicola: *I read recently in the press about your exciting new developments and your recent expansion. How can we help?*
>
> Buyer: *Yes, Nicola it is exciting, but it's also very chaotic at the moment. You can imagine the operational issues that we are dealing with, and that's having an effect on staff morale. We are currently operating under two different brand names, we have huge HR issues to resolve, 50 per cent of our workforce now have*

> *different contract terms, we have two uniforms at*
> *the moment, all of the systems have yet to be*
> *integrated and it will take us realistically a year to*
> *iron out all of these issues. Meanwhile I still need the*
> *team to be buzzed up.*

(Notice how he used the phrase 'I need the team buzzed up', whereas at this stage he is actually describing what he wants.)

Nicola: *So your main goal is to ensure everyone is buzzed*
up. Tell me, why is that important?

Buyer: *I suppose because it links back to the levels of*
customer service we deliver. If people are buzzed
up, they will give a better level of service to our
customers.

Nicola: *Why is that so important?*

Buyer: (He stops to think for a while then replies.)
We are in a tough market. If a potential customer
feels a bit off-colour it's possible to buy a bottle of
paracetamol almost anywhere, particularly in the
supermarket. We are proud of our local community
values, and we want to serve our local community,
so we want to create a service environment that if a
person within the footfall of one of our pharmacies
needs some pharmacy products they would rather
come to us because we care and that comes across
in the service we give.

Nicola: *So you want your people to be buzzed up, so*
they deliver great service, so your local customer
footfall will come to your stores for all their
pharmaceutical needs?

Buyer: Yes, yes that's it exactly.

Nicola: I know that all makes perfect business sense, but why specifically is that so important?

Buyer: It's about the targets, we have to hit the sales targets and we can't do that if we don't have customers in the store.

Nicola: Oh, OK. Now I appreciate how important this is, but I'm interested to know why hitting target is so crucial right now.

(By introducing the phrase 'right now' into the conversation at this point, I'm already beginning to create a sense of urgency in solving the client's problems.)

Buyer: (Again pauses to think then looks me directly in the eye.) *'Nicola, you don't even want to know how much we've borrowed to make this happen in the business and we absolutely must hit our targets, in order to fulfil our financial obligations on the interest alone!*

(Although I haven't yet uncovered his true emotional need, I know at this point I'm almost there. I've already uncovered much much deeper wants, bearing in mind his initial request was wanting his people to be 'buzzed up', yet by drilling down, I've already established much more specific outcomes this buyer desires.)

Nicola: Firstly I congratulate you on having the vision to take the necessary risks and I'm sure the long-term rewards will make all of this worthwhile, but let me ask another question. What does all of this really mean to you personally?

> *Buyer: Honestly ... this is my last chance to really make it happen and provide for myself and my family long-term ... it just can't fail.*

(Now we're getting somewhere!)

> *Nicola: So let me make sure I'm very clear. You need your people to be buzzed up, so that they deliver outstanding levels of customer service all of the time, so customers in your footfall always come to your pharmacies and choose you first, so that as a business owner you can feel confident that you will make the targets and fulfil your financial obligations and create the stable future you want?*

> *Buyer: Absolutely, I couldn't have put it any better myself.*

In the example above it's clear to see the difference between this client's wants and needs. He started the conversation by saying that he needed his team 'buzzed up' when in fact that is what he *wants* to happen. The reasons why this was so important were revealed after I had continued to drill down in the conversation. His real motivation was to provide for himself and his family well into the future – his driving emotional need is a feeling of long-term stability and financial security. So when I came to present my solution to this problem, I ensured that I linked our solution to fulfilling *this* need. Making his people buzzed up, which was his original request, was simply a positive by-product of the solution we proposed.

It would have been possible to build a proposition based on his first response or even the fact that he wanted his team to deliver great customer service, but without understanding his true driving emotional needs and no matter how brilliant the proposition I presented, it would never have been as compelling until it fulfilled his underlying need. I would have been left haphazardly chucking mud at the wall, hoping that some of it would stick.

Sales secret

◆ A client is only ever going to share their needs with you, if they feel in rapport and that they can trust you. Remember, by focusing on building trust, the client will answer all of your questions.

Their wounds

The conversation with this buyer did not stop here as the next part of the process is to uncover a buyer's wounds. Wounds are the potential outcomes that may result if the buyer does not take up your proposition (bearing in mind you haven't presented *any* solutions yet – you are still gathering information).

Remember the pain–pleasure equation we mentioned earlier in Chapter 4 – the buyer makes a commitment when they associate *more pain* with not buying. Therefore as part of your qualification process, you need to understand and appreciate what this potential sense of loss would mean to the client. This may seem a bit ruthless – why on earth would you want to make your buyer feel potential pain? This is simply because once they have understood the consequences of not buying from you they are extremely open to listening to your position – they will want to be healed at this point, and guess who happens to have a massive first-aid kit in their sales bag!

> ### Sales secret
>
> ◆ Uncovering wounds will require tact and skill. If you are too forceful, uncovering wounds can break rapport. Your client needs to feel that you are asking these questions because you ultimately want to help them and this information is important if you are going to be able to do that.

Here are a couple of examples of questions to ask in uncovering a buyer's wounds:

◆ *What could be the consequences of not . . . ?*

◆ *What would it mean if we didn't achieve . . . ?*

So continuing our buyer's conversation from before, let's uncover his wounds.

> Nicola: *So let me make sure I'm very clear. You need your people to be buzzed up, so that they deliver outstanding levels of customer service all the time, so customers in your footfall always come to your pharmacies and choose you first, so that as a business owner you can feel confident that you will make the targets and fulfil your financial obligations and create the stable future you want?'*
>
> Buyer: *Absolutely, I couldn't have put it any better myself.*

> *Nicola: I have one final question for you. What would be
> the consequences of NOT achieving this?*

When I asked this question, I slowed down my pace of
speech, looked him directly in the eye and used a tone of
voice that demonstrated I really appreciated his situation. At
this point the buyer didn't actually respond: I didn't need
him to. Instead he went very quiet whilst he reflected on the
question I had just asked. By simply asking the question, this
prompted him in his mind to realise that there could potentially be unpleasant consequences from his choices. I have
magnified the consequences of him not achieving his wants
and needs and have therefore magnified his desire to solve
these problems. I have increased his emotional attachment
to the outcome, increased his desire to buy and created
anticipation for a solution to his problems. His wounds are
now exposed and he is bleeding whilst he waits for me to
open my first-aid kit and apply a Band-Aid.

In this real-life example I actually went on in the conversation to link avoiding the consequences to buying my
proposition. I will explain how to do this in the next chapter;
however, first let's cover the final two areas of qualification
in the Hot Button – authority and resources.

Their authority

Obviously it makes sense to only deliver your sales proposition to the person or persons who will make the final buying
decision, and in an ideal world you would never take a meeting with anyone other than the decision maker. However, in
real life sometimes it is necessary to work your way up the
chain of command as you penetrate the buying chain.

Therefore, it is necessary to understand what level of authority you are dealing with *before you aim to close the deal*: that way you can tailor your presentation accordingly.

In my experience there are five main types of decision makers you may come across.

The Tea Boy: This in an affectionate term for the person who has been instructed to take your meeting but has absolutely no influence over the decision and they know it. They have simply been instructed to fob you off, or perhaps collect some information in the form of a proposal or a brochure.

An Influencer: This is a person who does not have the authority to say 'Yes' to the final decision, but does have the power, based on their recommendation, to put you in front of the decision maker. They can be disguised as a Personal Assistant, or a department assistant of some kind. They will have some knowledge of the wants and needs of the organisation and perhaps have been tasked with whittling down the first round of sales enquiries to two or three possible candidate companies. They could be a rising star in the company, which means they will have a strong desire to make wise choices that will improve their profile within the organisation. So by qualifying them you may find that their driving emotional need is a desire to look good in the eyes of their peers and their boss.

The Wannabe Decision Maker: This is the person who wishes they had the authority to make the decision, but they don't. However, they also don't want you to know that, so unless you qualify them correctly they will lead you to believe you are speaking to the decision maker, before slamming you with the classic 'I need to speak to my boss and come back to you' objection. In a business organisation they may be someone who has been there for a long time but everyone has been promoted above them, so their levels of authority have gradually diminished. They may be bitter about this and if so they will need to have their ego stroked.

A Joint Decision Maker: A Joint Decision Maker can sometimes pose problems, as unless you qualify them correctly they can lead you to believe that they have all of the authority to make the decision, yet before the final commitment can be made they need to gain the buy-in of a group. This could be a Board of Directors, a decision-making panel, a committee or even a husband and wife who want to make sure that the other party are completely comfortable with the overall decision before making the final commitment.

The Ultimate Decision Maker: As the description says, this is the person who has the final authority on the decision. By qualifying them as such, you know you can proceed to gain final commitment from this type of buyer. However, even though you may be presenting to an Ultimate Decision Maker, if you fail to qualify them you will have no way of knowing, meaning they would still have the opportunity to throw out a curve-ball objection later in the sales process if they did not want to proceed.

How to qualify the buyer's level of authority: Approached in the right way this is an easy area to qualify, but handled incorrectly this is another area that can lead to an instant

breakdown of rapport. The last thing you want to do is alien-
ate your buyer and make them feel inferior. We all like to be
validated by others, so it's important that you find ways to
qualify your client's buying power without making them feel
insignificant. The worst example I can remember of this
being handled badly was when someone asked 'So can you
write the cheque then?' Not a great example of professionally qualifying a buyer!

Here are some more refined questions you could ask:

◆ *Does anybody else need to be involved in making this decision?*

◆ *What would need to happen next in order to move ahead?*

◆ *What is the company procedure for the setting up of a new supplier?*

◆ *Are you in a position to make a commitment today?*

By asking any of these questions you will be able to identify
what the process would be in moving forward and if this
involves any committee or joint decisions. The examples on
the list are easy questions to ask anyone at any level within
an organisation and, most importantly, assume they have
some level of influence in the decision.

If at this stage it becomes obvious that you are not talking
to the Ultimate Decision Maker, then the whole purpose of
this interaction changes. When you are making an appointment the purpose of the phone call is *NOT* to sell your
product or service, but to *sell* the appointment. In this
instance, the purpose of your meeting now becomes selling a
further meeting which includes the Ultimate Decision
Maker. There is absolutely no point in trying as hard as you
can to close the sale if the prospect does not have the

authority to commit. It's a waste of your effort and at best you'll leave feeling confused and frustrated at their lack of commitment; at worst, you have lost control of the sale. You then become reliant on someone else to internally sell your proposition, someone who doesn't share your passion and enthusiasm or have your expert knowledge.

Sales secret

◆ Properly qualifying your buyer BEFORE presenting your sales proposition negates two of the most common objections 'refer to a higher authority' and 'let me think about it' later in the sale. If a client has confirmed they are able to make the buying decision today, the only way they can avoid making a decision at the point of commitment is by going back on their word – something that will feel uncomfortable for them and they are highly unlikely to want to do.

Their resources

Understanding the resources the client has available to them is the final element in clarifying the Hot Button, and this includes their financial situation. Obviously it's important to understand how much the client has available to spend, a question that is very rarely asked, usually because the salesperson feels uncomfortable asking about a client's financial circumstances. However, this is a big mistake. Unless you understand the client's buying situation you may be left justifying the cost of your product and you can walk slap bang into an objection – one that you've actually set up for the client! Get clarification on the client's finances, then everyone knows where they stand.

There are, however, other elements that also need to be considered as part of qualifying their resources. Depending on what you sell you may also need to consider the timescales for delivery, any level of commitment that may be required on the client's part in order to deliver the solution and perhaps even their cash-flow situation.

For example when I'm selling my consultancy services, I could be setting myself up for a big fat 'No' if I based my proposal simply on their wants, needs and wounds and came up with a solution that required 50% of the company's workforce to be taken offline for three weeks in order to be trained, if this is not workable in their business. If by asking these final questions it comes to light that the client can release their people in groups of 10, for 2 hours on a Friday afternoon, clearly I need to know this information, so that I can present my proposal in a way that fulfils these requirements. Without this level of clarification I would either lose the sale or seriously have to backtrack later and drastically change my solution when these restrictions come to light later on, perhaps in the form of a rejection.

Sales secret

◆ When you leave yourself with no option other than to radically change the delivery of your proposition, simply because you failed to qualify the client's resources properly, you massively reduce the credibility of your solution, never mind the dint you make in your own credibility.

Here are some example questions that will clarify the resources available:

◆ *Do you have a budget in mind?*

◆ *Are there any price guidelines I need to be aware of?*

◆ *What would need to happen next in order to move ahead?*

◆ *Do you have a figure in mind that you feel comfortable with?*

◆ *How much time are you able to commit to this project?*

◆ *Are there any restrictions or constraints that I'm not yet aware of that may affect the delivery of this project?*

◆ *Do you have a deadline I need to work to?*

What if they won't tell me their budget? Sometimes a client may be reluctant to share their budget with you: instead they may ask a question 'How much will it cost?' or 'I don't have a budget'. Their reasons for not wanting to share a budget with you can be varied. They may not have a lot of cash available to spend, but feel that sharing this will contradict the successful image they want to portray of their business – this is particularly relevant in smaller or start-up businesses, when the client always wants to portray a picture of a strong healthy growing business. Alternatively, they may feel that by giving you a budget, you will immediately hike your prices up and overcharge them.

If they express some reluctance to share their available spending with you, put them at ease and justify why sharing a budget with you will ultimately help them. Here are a couple of examples of how you can do this.

'I can understand your reluctance to tell me your available budget and that you may be concerned that I will immediately expect you to spend it all. However, we have a number of options and delivery solutions that could fulfil your requirements and it would simply be helpful to understand what resources you have available so that I don't suggest a solution with all the bells and whistles on, when we need to find an option that fulfils your need and at a price you can afford – which is why it is helpful to understand your available budget for this project.'

'For example, when you want to buy a car, you want a vehicle that will get you from A to B, therefore it maybe more important that we focus on the make, model and engine of the car; whereas if you had more available to spend you may choose to upgrade some of the extras such as including a 6-CD changer, SatNav and fit the car with bespoke wheels – which means you still get from A to B but you will enjoy the process more.'

OR

'For example, when you are choosing a dinner service you may want all 32 pieces available or simply a knife and fork that will get the job done.'

In both these examples you are alluding to the fact that your solution will deliver value for money – 'it will get you from A to B', 'a knife and fork that will get the job done' – but you are allowing for some flexibility in your solution depending on their available budget.

> *Sales secret*
>
> ◆ Sometimes a client simply won't tell you a budget in which case you will have to work without this information. In this instance you will need to test-close your proposition very carefully and pay close attention to their buying signals.

If, in response to your question about budget, they respond by asking your prices, deflect them until you have been able to establish their full needs, or give them a price range in your response, so that you avoid psychologically alienating them until you've the opportunity to present your Compelling Statement.

We do have a price list; however, we will compile a package that fits your needs and your budget. Do you mind if I ask you a few more questions?

Our service prices start from £1,500 and range to over £10,000 depending on what suits the client and their available budget. Do you mind if I ask you a few more quick questions?

Develop questions relevant to your business: Before you go any further, take your notebook and think of as many questions as possible that would be relevant to ask your type of buyer. Type them up on A4 sheets of paper and keep them at the front of your file, or stick them on the wall in front of your desk, so that you have them to hand when you are speaking to your clients. Eventually they will become second nature, but initially it helps to have the Hot Button framework at hand to ensure you correctly qualify every sales opportunity before you are tempted to sell your proposition.

Remember to remain disciplined in your approach: it's soooo tempting as you begin to use this technique and you start to uncover more detailed information about your client. Your instinct is to jump on the opportunity and start to sell; however, hold back until you are sure you have revealed the true Hot Button. Then and only then is it time to guide the sale forward by compelling the client to want to buy from you. Next you need to know how to...

7

Compel

NOW YOU HAVE CORRECTLY qualified the opportunity, it's time to present your solution, in a way that compels the client to want to commit to your opportunity and to do so with a sense of urgency. Therefore when you are building your compelling sales argument you need to accomplish two objectives:

1   Create momentum in the sale

2   Tailor your solution to fit the client's criteria

Creating momentum

A sales transaction is a two-way street between you and the customer. A game of racket ball is not very fulfilling if there is no one to catch the ball and throw it back. Therefore, at this stage it's important to clarify that the client is willing to participate in the game.

There is nothing more frustrating than ending a sales meeting with the client agreeing to your proposal yet failing to commit to the next steps! The easiest way to ensure you build momentum is to use a tie-down technique, which asks the client to make a commitment based on a set of conditions.

Remember that you still haven't presented your solution to their Hot Button needs, but before you reveal your hand it's obviously prudent to make it clear that you have an expectation that the customer will deal, assuming of course that all their conditions are fulfilled.

Here are some real-life examples of tie-downs and the context within which they have been used.

'If we get the deal right, can we have the business?'

This is a brilliant quote to use once you have summarised the information revealed by the client's Hot Button. It is the next phrase I used in our previous example with the pharmaceutical buyer.

> *Nicola: So let me make sure I'm very clear. You need your people to be buzzed up, so that they deliver outstanding levels of customer service all the time, so customers in your footfall always come to your pharmacies and choose you first, so that as a business owner you can feel confident that you will make the targets and fulfil your financial obligations and create the stable future you want?*
>
> *Buyer: Absolutely, I couldn't have put it any better myself.*
>
> *Nicola: I have one final question for you. What would be the consequences of NOT achieving this?*

(Pause as client contemplates the question that has just been asked.)

> *Nicola: OK, so if we get the deal right, can we have the business?*
>
> *Buyer: Yes, definitely.*

By using this tie-down in the conversation, I have already gained a commitment from the client based on the condition of 'getting the deal right'. However, I have also allowed for some flexibility when delivering my proposal. If I don't get the deal right first time, I have allowed myself the opportunity to refine the proposition until it meets the client's needs, yet I have gained their commitment that they are prepared to work with us. Remember, I still haven't given them any indication of *how* I will fulfil their needs; nevertheless they have now shown their commitment to work with us.

If the word 'deal' makes you feel uncomfortable and wouldn't fit your style of selling then simply substitute it with an alternative: 'proposal', 'solution', 'options'. For example; 'If we can show you the option that feels right for you, can we agree that you will work with us?'

Here are some further examples.

> *'If you like what we discuss today, can we agree a further meeting with yourself and the **Ultimate Decision Maker**?'*

This is clearly useful if you discover that you are not presenting to the decision maker and you need to gain commitment that you can come back and re-present your opportunity.

> *'Assuming when we meet up I can substantiate everything that we have discussed today over the telephone, will you be in a position to make a commitment and sign the paperwork?'*

This is a prudent tie-down to use when you have qualified your prospect but wish to ensure the client is committed before you expend any additional time and resource.

Rob Bell is an extraordinary salesperson. As well as being a master sales professional, like many sales people he has huge pressures on his time. I worked with Rob many years ago and always admired his level of laser-sharp focus and commitment. He now works for a revolutionary firm in the financial sector which is shaking up the way in which the industry currently serves its customers. Rob's role as Recruitment Director involves persuading the right kind of financial services professional to join their ranks. This means that Rob's target customer could be based geographically anywhere in the country and therefore it's imperative that he correctly qualifies *and* creates a sense of urgency with his prospects before he drives a 600-mile round trip, only to discover the client was simply curious about what he had to say.

Here is an example of Rob's tie-down technique:

'On the basis that I can demonstrate that everything we discuss is true, and I answer all of your questions in a totally transparent manner, bearing in mind that this is the best proposition in the market place today, when we meet up are you willing to make a commitment there and then and sign up? It's simply not worth both of us giving up a day of our time if you're not entirely sure.'

This may seem a tough approach, but Rob's conversions are amazing – why? Simply because he'd rather spend his time focusing on serious sales opportunities and any prospects who are not quite ready; he allows them time to mature before he takes them on to the next level. However, by being this upfront and being prepared to walk away from prospects who are not prepared to commit *before* he overloads them with benefits and reasons to buy, he leaves them wanting to know more. He appeals to their sense of loss, which actually has the effect of making his proposition even more attractive! Those clients who may have been teetering on the edge are more likely to say 'Yes' simply because their sense of loss kicks in and they don't want to miss out.

It's a bit like taking the dog to the park and then when it's time to go home you chase him around for hours trying to get his collar on, yet the minute you turn your back and start to walk away shouting a nonchalant 'I'm off home for dinner, are you coming?' the dog suddenly comes running after you!

Rob told me recently 'I'm not in the habit of wasting my time or the company's resources on a wild-goose chase. I want to know that they're serious before I commit myself to the meeting.'

Building a compelling proposition

Finally, after all of the rapport-building, engaging, qualifying and creating momentum, you are going to tell the client *how* you can solve their problems and provide a suitable solution. **Now and only now are you actually going to sell!**

By spending so much of your effort in the earlier stages of the sales process, you are now in a very strong position to sell the most suitable solution that will press the client's Hot Button. It's time to design a solution that fits your client's criteria.

> *Sales secret*
>
> ◆ Many salespeople fail to tailor their sales proposition
>   and dish out the same sales spiel to every customer.
>   However, we are all individuals motivated by different
>   desires: therefore, as a customer we need to feel as
>   though your solution has been tailored to fit our needs.
>
> ◆ If you present benefits that do not match the client's
>   emotional needs you may still win the business, but it
>   will be by default as opposed to guidance from yourself.

The Compelling Statement

In Chapter 4 you were asked to list your product features,
their associated benefits and how these benefits will make
your prospects feel. Now we simply need to apply them to a
structure that conveys the most suitable benefits to the customer: you need to design your Compelling Statement which
has four components. First we give the client a Recommendation, followed by a Feature, which converts into a Benefit
for the client, before finally associating a further Benefit
which links back to their emotional attachment to the sale –
what they want to feel as an outcome of taking the risk.

When designing a relevant Compelling Statement, work
backwards. First choose a Benefit that will fulfil the emotional need of the client, then decide what would be the
Feature of that benefit and finally how that converts into a
Recommendation. Once you have decided on the most relevant information, use the following structure to compile it
into a coherent format.

◆ Make your *recommendation*

◆ Based on one of the product's *features*

◆ Because it has an associated *benefit*

◆ Then stack on an additional *benefit* that relates to the buyer's emotional need to make the recommendation even more compelling.

Here are some examples of how to structure a Compelling Statement. Let's assume that this client has enquired about a coaching programme and while uncovering the Hot Button we identified their underlying need is 'peace of mind'.

> *'I recommend our professional 1–1 coaching programme as it allows us to tailor the programme to your specific business needs, which means we will be on hand to react to anything that may arise unexpectedly in your business, which means you will always have peace of mind that you will receive the professional support you need, when you need it most.'*

Have you spotted the structure? First we make the recommendation of 'our professional 1–1 coaching programme' because of the feature that 'it will allow us to tailor the programme to your specific business needs', then by using the phrase 'which means', we can introduce our first benefit 'we will be on hand to react to anything that may arise unexpectedly in your business', before stacking on an additional benefit that appeals to this buyer's emotional need 'you will always have peace of mind'.

Here is another example: except this client wants to experience value for money and validation that they have made the right choice.

> *'I recommend this "make and model". It is our bestseller because it offers such good value for money, which means you know you've got a great deal and the fact that it is so popular with so many other customers means you can feel secure that you'll have made a wise choice.'*

Here are a few more examples.

> *'I recommend you sign up as a committed donor to our charity which will allow you to make smaller regular donations, which means it's easier for you to keep track and it's easier for us to manage our charity, so we would both be helping each other, which as an existing supporter I know feels important to you.'*

> *'I suggest you place a slightly larger order for 'x' volume because by agreeing to that shipment it will allow us some flexibility on our pricing structure, which means overall you would be receiving better value on each item – which means more profit potential, as I know how important making this business successful means to you.'*

That really is all there is to it! You've done it, you've successfully presented your sales proposition. So many people lack confidence in selling, because they feel it's complicated or beyond their capabilities; however, when you break it down in this way and follow a simple structure such as this, any time you need to influence others you can structure your argument that presents the opportunity for them in this compelling way.

> *'Could we reschedule our finance meeting to next Tuesday afternoon? I've checked our diaries and we are both free and by then I will have had more time to work on the figures, which means I know I will have all the information you need to hand and I will have had time to double-check its accuracy, which means we won't have to come back and revisit anything which is more likely if we had the meeting this afternoon.'*

> *'Let's focus on getting the garden weeded and the grass cut on Saturday morning, because then the children will be able to play outside, which means they will have room to burn off some energy, which means they won't trash the house, and it will leave us some time and space to enjoy a bit of peace and quiet knowing they are playing safely outside.'*

As you can see from the statements above, Compelling Statements are really useful in lots of scenarios, not just the classic sales conversation. They can be used anywhere, in fact whenever you need to influence someone else.

Design your own Compelling Statements that are relevant to you and the scenarios you need to influence others. Take your notebook and following the structure above write out five examples of Compelling Statements that would be relevant to your business or sales proposition.

So what?

A great way of ensuring you are presenting Benefits, not just stating Features, is to use the 'So what?' check in your head.

If, after you've presented your Compelling Statement, you cannot find a compelling answer to the question 'So what?', then the chances are you are still stating Features and haven't converted them into Benefits – a highly common mistake that even the most seasoned professional sometimes still makes.

◆ *This car is highly fuel efficient* – So what?

◆ *We have that suit in your size* – So what?

◆ *We can customise our delivery to suit your needs* – So what?

◆ *That's the latest model; it's just been released* – So what?

◆ *It's made of the finest materials* – So what?

◆ *We offer outstanding levels of quality and service* – So what?

It's such an easy trap to fall into. I love being visited by sales-people who are clearly experts in their field and *really* listening to how they present their products. So many of them present their products with such passion, enthusiasm and knowledge, yet fail to state a single benefit in their conversation.

Even though it is easy to see the obvious benefits that follow on from the features in the statements above, if you do not clearly present the benefits that link to your client's emotional needs (not just their wants), you are leaving them to bridge that gap on their own. You have stopped guiding the conversation and have lost control of the sale. Your only hope is to assume that they create in their mind the links to the benefits that will fit their criteria. And if they don't, they will walk away and you may be left bewildered and wondering why.

Here are some of the Compelling Statements from earlier, only with the benefits removed.

'I recommend our professional 1–1 coaching programme as it allows us to tailor the programme to your specific business needs.'

'I recommend you sign up as a committed donor to our charity which will allow you to make smaller regular donations.'

'I suggest you place a slightly larger order for "x" volume because by agreeing to that shipment it will allow us some flexibility on our pricing structure.'

H'm. These examples are not nearly as compelling as when the benefits are clearly stated.

Take the opportunity to review company literature and websites and count how many benefits you can read in the first few paragraphs. I suspect that in most other organisations you will find lots of features listed, for example: we do this, we're great at that, here is a list of our satisfied customers; if you were a customer reading it, all the while you could quite simply be thinking 'So what?' It may seem obvious but just remember to link the most appropriate benefits to your client's criteria, and in the case of company literature, to your ideal client's needs.

Using visual aids

We've all sat through some dreadful presentations in our time, delivered by a boring presenter who added no value and you leave the meeting wishing they had simply emailed you the information or sent you their brochure as you wouldn't have wasted your time turning up! Likewise we have also experienced a refreshing sales presentation delivered in a confident, professional manner, which was engaging, informative and left you wanting more. So what is it that makes the difference? Apart from the delivery style and confidence of the presenter, very often it was the quality of the sales aids and how they were used.

At most sales meetings I attend, particularly initial meetings with only one buyer, I walk in with a blank piece of paper and a pen and simply draw any points I want to make to the client. I tend not to use visual aids unless a second meeting is required and only then if absolutely necessary. However, there will always be situations where it is more appropriate to prepare a sales presentation using more stimulating visual aids, or refer to your brochure, catalogue or website; like most skills, there are successful tricks you can use that will ensure you increase your impact. Get it wrong and you will bore the pants off your customer, make yourself look foolish and screw up your chances of winning the sale – therefore you need to know how to use visual aids in a way that makes your message even more compelling.

If you are using prepared visual aids, no matter what the format, follow the sales structure that has been outlined thus far. So ensure you have the buyer engaged, you have built strong rapport and you have properly qualified the opportunity before you pull out any brochures. If you start a sales conversation and lead with the brochure, all the client's focus will be on the brochure and they will not be listening to any questions you may be asking or they will switch off from anything you say. In short they are disengaged.

My friend Colin Kendall is the founder and Managing Director of 7Presentations, a company which offers services that improve the impact of people's presentations. Not surprisingly Colin's sales *secret* is to ensure people really understand your proposition and he achieves this by creating and using highly professional visual aids.

In order to do this you need to understand the fundamentals of using visual aids in a way that adds impact to your message, and not fall into the trap of *thinking* you are using aids that add impact but actually distract the buyer.

The biggest mistake that people often make when compiling a sales presentation is that, instead of preparing material that supports their delivery, they compile a presentation that substitutes their presence!

Sales secret

◆ Visual aids should substantiate your message through the use of colours, shapes, images and movement. They should not be a duplication of your message in text format.

A person can read five times faster than they can listen, so if all the information you were going to say is presented to the client in text format, in order to read the information you've given them they have to stop listening to you. They will be aware that you are speaking, but their focus is on reading the text and they will not hear what you've just said.

Have you ever experienced the 'deer in the headlights' look from someone? This occurs when they are looking at you, but their mind is focused elsewhere. Their expression will be blank and their eyes unfocused. If this happens you need to re-engage their focus and regain control of the conversation, and the easiest way to do so is by asking a question.

If you are using visual computer software, such as Microsoft PowerPoint, avoid using the inbuilt templates, which simply encourage you to write a bulleted list of the points you wish to talk through. Instead these should be your *speaker notes* and *NOT* used as a visual representation of your message. Think about how your message can be translated into a visual image and build a slide that delivers that. Likewise if you have a company brochure or catalogue, turn to the pages with graphs, maps and images of your product; avoid allowing the customer to read the text in the brochure which turns their attention away from you.

For example, here is a PowerPoint slide from one of my seminar talks.

This is the supportive slide I use to illustrate the point that 'people make their buying decisions based on emotion and then justify those decisions with logic'. By using animation, I can also increase the impact of what I'm saying by *revealing* the associated image at the point I say the words. That way the person listening associates what they hear with what they see. The smiley face represents emotion and the tick board obviously represents logic.

Technically this is what is called 'opening the loop' in the client's mind. When I show the picture of the smiley face, it presents the client's brain with information that, as yet, has no meaning. It opens a loop, and we all want to understand what we see. We want to associate *meaning* with the image. When this happens the client becomes completely focused on what you are saying as they need you to reveal the missing information that gives meaning to the picture. Clever, eh?!

Think about how you can remain engaged with a movie for 90 minutes or more. All the way through they *reveal* the next part of the story which keeps you hooked until the end. Likewise, how frustrating if you work the plot out within the first 10 minutes and there are no more surprises revealed; you may sit through until the end, but you are less engaged and have a lower opinion of the movie's quality.

This technique will make the difference between correctly using visual aids to increase the impact of your message or thoroughly boring the buyer. The slide above, for example, is much more engaging than the example below, which could be used to make the same point.

•People make their buying decisions based on emotion

•And then justify them with logic

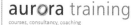 aurora training
courses, consultancy, coaching

 nicolacook
keynote & motivational speaker

Here are some final Dos and Don'ts to consider when using visual aids to compel your buyer.

Do:

◆ Hold handouts until the end of the meeting.

◆ Find ways to convert your message into pictorial and imagery formats.

◆ Use colours, shapes and movement to build on your message as you speak.

◆ Reveal information as you talk through your presentation as opposed to presenting all the visual information at once. Retain control of a document or brochure by turning the pages as you speak, as opposed to handing the document to the buyer.

◆ Keep it simple. They are not buying your ability to prepare a highly complicated visually dynamic presentation: they want to know about your product and service and how this relates to them.

◆ Get there early if you need to set up the meeting room. It's not professional to be crawling under the table trying to find an electrical socket if the room is already full of buyers. Make friends with the gatekeeper and they will help you.

◆ Make sure all your equipment, samples and laptops (including the screen!) are clean before you use it to deliver a presentation. The remnants of last night's dinner smeared all over the keyboard of your computer will cause the buyer to form a negative judgement of you, which will simply create an unnecessary barrier to the sale.

◆ Practise, practise and practise some more until you are sure your delivery supported with visual aids is super slick, otherwise you'd be better off without them rather than deliver an overall poor presentation.

◆ Invest time and money in learning presentation skills, especially in how to deliver professional presentations if this is something you do on a regular basis.

Don't:

◆ Use your sales presentation as speaker notes.

◆ Ever rely solely on technology to deliver your message. You need to be able to generate the same impact, even if the power is out (which has happened to me!).

- Overcomplicate your slides and kill off your buyer, something that is known in the industry as 'Death by PowerPoint'. As a rule of thumb, use no more than 10 words per slide (if you are using a visual package such as PowerPoint).

- Blame the technology: you chose to use it, so if you blame a poor presentation on the technology, it only reflects poorly on you.

- Stand in front of an image if it is being projected. I know this may seem obvious, but you will be amazed how many people, once they get going, are unaware that their body image is casting a shadow over the presentation!

- Be afraid to ditch the visual aids part-way through a presentation if they stop adding value, and the client simply wants to engage in a conversation.

By now your client should feel compelled by your propositions and ready to ...

8
Commit

YOU'VE DONE ALL THE HARD WORK so make sure you don't walk away without asking for the order – you'd be amazed how many people do! It's time now to gain the client's commitment.

As well as knowing the most effective ways of asking for the business, you also need to ensure you close the business and agree they will buy *now*, not long off into the future. The first part of effectively closing the business is ensuring you understand *when* to ask for the order, which means you need to be able to *read* your buyer.

Failing to do this effectively could create that uncomfortable situation that comes when a salesperson asks for commitment too early and the buyer is not quite ready to say 'Yes'. It breaks rapport and leads to a long pause or silence. Even if a buyer was almost on the tipping point of saying 'Yes', asking for the commitment too soon is more likely to make them say 'No'. Likewise it is equally unprofessional *NOT* asking for the business at the most appropriate time. If your client is ready to buy, eager to give you their commitment, and their credit card is burning a hole in their back pocket and you don't ask for the business, they will become equally frustrated and could walk away!

Perk up your Scooby Ears

Scooby Ears is the phrase I use to describe using what's known as your sensory acuity, which is the acute use of all of your senses to appreciate the other person's feelings and thoughts. As you proceed through a sales conversation, your buyer will be absorbing the information and associating their own meaning to your messages, obviously guided by your now improved sales skills! Get it right and they will be compelled to buy as they associate strong emotions to your sales proposition; get it wrong and they will be disengaged and uninterested in your offer. Your job is to judge their thinking and choose the most appropriate time to guide them into making a commitment to the proposition.

The term Scooby Ears comes from the cartoon character Scooby Doo. As a child I was a big fan and would eagerly switch on every day to watch Scooby and the gang solve the mystery. The plot always followed the same format and reached a point where Shaggy was being dragged backwards into a cupboard by the Ghost, which was usually the Caretaker in disguise! (I was about 10 years old when I sussed that one out.) Anyway, at this exact point in the plot Scooby would prick up his ears and make his trademark Scooby grunt as he tried in vain to alert the other members of the gang to the impending danger. In that moment Scooby Doo 'got it'. His sensory acuity was telling him something was up. As a sales professional, you need to ensure your Scooby Ears are perked up and *reading* the signals that your buyer is giving off as they interpret your sales proposition and place their own meaning on the opportunity you're presenting.

Sales secret

◆ It is possible to lose a sale, even after a perfect execution simply by not correctly reading your buyer. So ensure your Scooby Ears are perked up and you pick up on the relevant signals.

Remember that from the very first contact you make with a person and long after they've said 'Yes' to the sale, they are continuously managing the delicate balancing act in their mind *'Which is more painful: the pain of taking the risk and agreeing to the sale, or the pain of missing out and walking away?'* Very often they would be persuaded by the argument in one moment and then in the next their opinion could sway the other way. Clearly, it makes sense to ask for their commitment when the buying pendulum is swayed in your favour.

Your buyer will give off signals that with your Scooby Ears perked up, will help you judge your buyer's emotional position. Obviously if you are face to face with a client then you will be able to read their body language, but even if you are over the phone there are still clues in their behaviour that will guide you.

They use language as if they've already purchased: As a customer just before you make a decision to purchase, you imagine what it would be like to own the product and live with it. Therefore if a client starts to either ask questions or use language which relate to their circumstances *after* they've made the purchase, then you can assume that they are associating in their mind how it will feel once they own the product or the service. Mentally they are trying it on for size to see how it fits and this is a solid indication they are thinking about making the commitment.

They change to a more positive tone: Initially as you are building rapport and asking questions the client may appear guarded and reluctant to demonstrate their trust in you, particularly if it is the first time they have met you or spoken with you. If, however, they like what you have said and the way in which you have said it, they will begin to show their change of opinion and lighten up. The tone in their voice becomes friendlier, their body language will become more relaxed and they will appear less guarded.

They ask more detailed questions about the product features and benefits: If they weren't interested they wouldn't ask any questions, whereas if they are interested but not completely convinced that there is value in it for them, they will want to know more. In this case, make sure you continue to present only features and benefits that relate to their Hot Button. If you feel you need to dig deeper, turn their enquiry into a question back to them. 'I'm interested to know, what specifically made you ask about that?' and you may find you uncover more wants, needs and wounds. Keep your answers simple and stick to the Compelling Statement structure so you don't bamboozle them with information that is not relevant.

Alternatively, another way to build more conviction into the sale on the back of a client question is to relate their question to another person's experience. By telling someone's personal experience, you are making the client feel certain that they are making the right choice. This is the perfect way to introduce other client testimony into the sales process. Third-party endorsements add credibility and clout to the claims you've made thus far.

Think of the teleshopping channels: all the products sold in this way usually carry a celebrity endorsement followed by lots and lots of 'ordinary' people's positive experiences, people just like you and me. By associating with them and their experiences, we automatically begin to believe how the product will also benefit us. I carry with me what I called a 'Brag file', which I keep in my briefcase, of glowing client testimony and positive PR on our company to show prospective clients, but only if necessary.

They enquire about the next steps in the sales process: This could be mistakenly interpreted as a sign of low conviction. If they begin to enquire about the actions they themselves need to take in order to start gaining the benefits, this actually demonstrates interest. Depending on how they ask the next steps question, it is possible to turn their interest into an immediate tie-down that leads directly into a closing commitment.

This is illustrated by the following two examples.

Client: *Could you deliver by Tuesday?*
Salesperson: *Would you like delivery on Tuesday?*

Client:	*Yes.*
Salesperson:	*OK, great, we'll get delivery sorted by Tuesday.*
Or	
Client:	*What are my payment options?*
Salesperson:	*What would be your preferred payment options?*
Client:	*Could I pay over 6 months?*
Salesperson:	*No problem, we can do that. I'll get the paperwork sorted now.*

In both these examples you can easily see how straightforward it is to turn their questions into a tie-down which leads directly into a commitment, rather than simply answering their direct question with a simple 'Yes' response.

Pace and Lead: In Chapter 5 we covered how to build rapport with your client so that they feel more comfortable with you. So another clue to watch out for is the presence of Pace and Lead between you and the key decision maker. If they begin to follow your body language, then they are sending an unconscious signal that they trust you, they believe what you are saying and want you to feel an affinity with them.

You can test Pace and Lead in the conversation if you are unsure. Change your body stance, cross or uncross your legs, shift your weight, or listen out for any phrases the buyer may use in their language which were initiated by you.

They ask questions about you personally: The final signal that can demonstrate their interest is if they start to ask you personal questions or draw you into a personal conversation. If they weren't interested in buying they wouldn't be interested in you. However, remember that people only buy from people they like, so by asking more personal questions they are wanting to get to know *you* better.

They may enquire about your reasons for joining the company, or your background before that, your personal relationship, whether you have children, what sporting team you support: in fact anything that does not relate to the company, the business scenario or the product sale!

Sales secret

◆ It's much easier to read the buyer when you can be objective and professional. If you are emotionally attached to closing this one sale – say, for example, you are desperate to close just this one opportunity in order to make your monthly target – instead of focusing on your buyer, your desperation will cloud your head and you are likely to miss some vital clues.

In all of the scenarios above, these are all positive signals that the buyer is showing interest in your proposition. If you combine these positive buying signals with a Test Close you will be able to ensure your client is piping hot before you ask for their final commitment.

Creating a 'Yes' momentum

Using a series of Test Closes allows you to build the level of commitment in the sale by creating a 'Yes' momentum. The technical difference between a Test Close and a Close in the sales process is that a Test Close ask for the buyer's opinion, whereas a close is a decision-making question. Therefore it is possible to use the test-closing technique wherever you feel you need to confirm the buyer's opinion without the risk of potential rejection. Here are some examples:

- *'How does that sound?'*

- *'How does that look to you?'*

- *'How does this feel?'*

- *'Is that something that you feel would be useful?'*

- *'Can you see yourself using this?'*

- *'If we could find a way to deal with that, would you be willing to go ahead with an order today?'*

- *'Do you like the look of what we have presented here today?'*

- *Which is more attractive: Option A or Option B?'*

All of the above answers (with the exception of the last one) guide the client to say 'Yes'. In this scenario it's unlikely they will give you a flat 'No' even if they are unsure, but by asking for their opinion it gives you an opportunity to read their buying position. Also by guiding the client to say 'Yes' multiple times, it generates a Yes momentum. By agreeing with you at each stage of the sales process, it builds belief in the client's mind that your proposition will benefit them, so finally when you do ask them for their commitment it will feel uncomfortable and odd for them to say 'No'.

One word of warning – there is no definitive correct number of Test Closes to use in a sales conversation: however, if they are overused, the client may begin to feel manipulated. Instead find ones that suit your style, use your natural tone of voice, be relaxed, build them into the conversation and combine the use of your Scooby Ears and you can't come unstuck. Use an obvious Test Close after every statement and fail to read the other buying signals and you may risk breaking rapport and alienating the client.

Positioning your value proposition

Unless you've covered the price of your product as part of your Compelling Statement or it is listed in your brochure, you may find that you haven't yet covered the price the client will need to pay for your services. If this is the case, they are likely to ask at this stage, yet remember this is actually a demonstration of their interest. If they weren't interested in buying they wouldn't ask.

Now, if you've followed the Hot Button technique correctly you should have established the client's budget, so will already know what the client can afford. In which case, simply state your prices: 'That option will cost "x"'. Regardless of their available budget, you must remember to state your price with firm confidence. If you show *any* hint that you do not believe that the price represents value, or indicate that you are bracing yourself for an objection, your client will pick up on it straightaway and you will inadvertently transfer that lack of belief into their thinking.

I had a client who had a real problem stating her prices with confidence. Every time she laid out her price plan, she screwed her face up and pulled an expression as though she was bracing herself for a rejection. Clearly pulling this face was not going to instil belief in her prospective clients that she was offering great value for money. By digging a bit deeper, it became evident that she linked the value of her services with her own perceptions of her personal self-worth. Until she believed she was worth that amount, she was never going to convince a buyer to part with that amount of cash.

Sales secret

◆ People buy based on their 'perception of value', not the price.

If the buyer hasn't given you a budget or was unwilling to share their budget with you earlier, you may find yourself working blind at this point. However, don't panic: still state your prices with pride; just make sure that you have used a Test Close following your Compelling Statement and are confident that they are demonstrating positive buying signals. You will also need to use your Scooby Ears and perhaps a further Test Close to find out how they feel about your value proposition after you've stated your price.

'That option only requires an investment of "X". How does that fit with your budget?'

Depending on their response you may have to think on your feet as, if you find you are clearly way out, you don't want to appear to simply slash your price to win the business, as this will imply that there was plenty of margin in your initial costing. If they show any resistance to your initial price, before repositioning your prices, you absolutely must ask them their available budget. Another option in this situation is to include an additional product or value into the package, thus increasing the overall value of the proposition. Or if you do offer a discount, ensure that it is linked to a timeframe which accelerates the sale process and requires them to make a firm commitment.

Sales secret

◆ There is no point offering a discount unless it offers benefit to both sides and requires the client to make a firm commitment.

The following is an example:

Salesperson: *That option only requires an investment of £2,000. How does that fit with your budget?*

Client: *H'm. It's more than I was thinking of paying.*

Salesperson: *OK. So can you tell me your maximum available spend? / What are you able to sign off today?*

Client: *£1,700.*

Salesperson: *OK, great. If I am able to find a way to match your budget, would you be willing to agree a start date for the project today?*

Client: *Yes.*

(Note: if they were to say 'No' at this point, revert back to Resource qualification from the Hot Button and perhaps ask a different question 'OK, so what would need to happen now in order for us to move ahead?')

Salesperson: *In which case I would be glad to offer you a 15% discount, providing you place the order today.*

I had this exact scenario with a new client I've just acquired this week. During the initial conversation with the buyer's Personal Assistant to set up the appointment, I was asked to list our prices and managed to deflect the question until meeting the buyer face to face. During my Hot Button questioning I was unable to clarify a budget so had to state my prices blind. My Test Close revealed that I was over their available budget, but we both still wanted to agree the contract and move ahead, so I had a choice to make about how to handle the situation.

This client in itself presented a huge opportunity for my business; it was one of our target blue-chip customers and this opportunity presented a way to get my foot in the door, so it was worth sacrificing margin to close the deal. I had to make the call between agreeing the business there and then, or risk forcing this buyer to go further up the chain of command to get additional sign-off, which would mean losing control of the sales process with no guarantee of even winning the business.

So after clarifying how much the buyer was able to sign off and had the available budget for, we were able to strike a deal that both of us felt comfortable with, which did not damage my overall value proposition. By the way, I will ensure that we deliver a full-value solution as if they had still paid the full price. Personally I do not sacrifice quality over cost saving so, by delivering outstanding value for money, I am confident they will already have experienced massive value in our services when I want to increase my prices in the future.

> *Sales secret*
>
> ◆ Less than 15% of people will only ever buy the cheapest available option. That is why branded products automatically carry a *perception* of higher value, and can therefore charge a higher premium. So, providing you can demonstrate value in your proposition your client will justify any additional cost.

Finally if you have managed to acquire a budget from your client but it falls short of your prices, you can trust that they will find the additional resources to complete the sale if you are absolutely certain you can demonstrate value in your proposition and they are able to associate massively with the outcomes. My advice is always to continue presenting the opportunity even if their available budget falls 25% below your price list.

If your business strategy is always based on being the cheapest and you offer the client no value, then you are in danger of eroding your brand and potentially your industry value, as other competitors undercut you to win back business and so the vicious cycle continues until virtually no margin remains in your business model.

There are some industries that have persistently used this strategy to effectively 'buy' new business by enticing clients away from their competitors, only to lose them when the customer seeks to renew their services. By using this strategy they have educated the consumer to 'shop around' for the best deal. Some examples that spring to mind are: credit cards, utilities such as gas and electricity, mortgages, mobile phones, office stationery supplies, some household furniture retailers, particularly sofa retailers, and travel suppliers. Although reducing prices may win business in the short term, in the long term it erodes brand value and builds absolutely no brand loyalty.

By all means use 'loss leaders' to win initial business if the client will offer long-term value, but don't be drawn into an ongoing cost-cutting strategy. Instead, find ways to offer the client value in your proposition, focus on targeting your ideal customer and make sure you properly qualify your opportunities.

Sales secret

◆ This is a great question to ask yourself, to ensure you always sell with both a short-term and long-term focus:

'If we didn't need the money from this sale, would this still be a good deal for the customer and our business?'

Asking for the business

'Closing the sale' – three words that can strike fear into even the most confident of sales professionals, yet, hopefully, by now you should realise that if you follow all the steps that have been laid out in the previous chapters, you should never find yourself in a situation where you are asking for the business and expecting anything other than a 'Yes'.

However, unless the client has directly asked you to place the order, you will still need to gain their final commitment and ask for the business. There are two easy ways to do this and one method that I strongly discourage. Let's look at the two simple methods first.

1   The Assumptive Close

2   The Alternative Close

Assuming the sale

The Assumptive Close does exactly what it says on the tin – you simply assume the sale. If you have followed the previous steps through correctly and particularly if you have used a Tie-down and Test Close and they have confirmed their interest, then don't faff about any more: just assume that they are in agreement and guide them smoothly and swiftly through the final stages of the sales process.

> *'Great. That's all sorted now. What will happen next is ...'*

> *'Fantastic. We'll get that ordered now. I just need to run through some paperwork with you.'*

Some people feel uncomfortable taking this level of control at this point in the sale, effectively not giving the client *any* opportunity to back out. But remember, if you have followed all the previous stages verbatim you would never be in a situation where you would ever have to ask for business and not expect a positive outcome. The other great method to smooth through the commitment stage is to use the Alternative Close.

Offering alternatives

Here you can offer the client two alternatives, both resulting in a sale; you are simply asking them which option they wish to confirm.

'That's great. Would you prefer delivery on Tuesday morning or afternoon?'

'That's great. Would you prefer option A or our best value option B?'

Both options require a commitment to the sale; you are simply giving the client the choice as to which option they would prefer. A few extra points to consider here are: always state the option you would prefer them to choose as option B. Therefore it is the last thing they hear and is therefore more likely to be the first point they will recall. If your second choice is the more expensive option, insert a phrase such as 'best value', 'family-sized' or 'combined package' which assumes a higher value in the more expensive option.

It is also possible to combine both of these two techniques to assume the sale and then use options as a way of clarifying a point, such as payment.

'Great, that's all confirmed now. Would you prefer to pay via Visa or MasterCard?'

How simple is that! One final watch-out, however – never use an Alternative Close where you give the client the option of *not* buying: 'That's great. Would you like me to go ahead, *or not?*' After all of the hard work you've put in using these skills – building rapport, properly qualifying the opportunity, and presenting your Compelling Statements – why on earth would you offer the client the option to NOT buy now?

> *Sales secret*
>
> ◆ At the point of commitment in the sale, avoid giving the
> client any options that could result in rejection.

Previously in my career when I managed a large telesales
team, I had one guy who was an absolutely brilliant salesperson, but right at the end of his sales presentation he would
use this statement and give the client the option *not to buy*. It
had become habitual and most of the time he wasn't even
aware he was saying it. So one day I stood behind him and
tickled him (I must admit the tickles turned into playful
slaps by the end of the day!) every time he offered the client
an option of not buying. It only took one day of tickles and
ruffled hair, but eventually we managed to break his habit
and his sales results flew through the roof.

Avoid closed questions

The only method of gaining commitment that I strongly recommend you avoid is the direct closing method where you
ask a closed question, which again can be answered with a
Yes/No answer.

'Would you like me to place the order?'

'Do you want to go ahead?'

Just as in the previous example, **avoid any scenario** where
you give the client the option of turning you down.

Congratulate them and agree the next steps

So hooray, finally you have agreed the sale and the client has committed to your offer. Take the time now to make them feel good about their decision. Think about it. In order to agree to the sale, not only have they had to believe you, but they've had to place their belief in the proposition you've presented and perhaps (particularly if your sale is a concept sell and they won't gain any benefit until after delivery of the service) they haven't had the opportunity to gain from the benefits you've presented. They've just bought you, so make sure you thank them!

Right now, they need to feel certain that they've made a good decision. So before you start talking detail or logistics, or become buried in paperwork and purchase orders, look them directly in the eye, shake their hand and say something that will make them feel even more certain that they've made the right choice.

> *'Thank you. I really appreciate your belief in me.*
> *We will deliver you an awesome solution; I know you*
> *won't be disappointed.'*

> *'I am so pleased you've agreed to partner with us.*
> *I will personally ensure you continue to feel this*
> *satisfied with your decision, long into the future of our*
> *working relationship.'*

Even if you are not face to face with your client and you are either in telesales or closing a deal over the telephone, take the time to congratulate the buyer and make them feel good about their choice.

Finally before you leave the conversation, outline all of the next steps that the client can expect, what paperwork they will be sent, when they will receive delivery. Make them aware of any other departments within your organisation that they may need to liaise with and ensure that they can reach you personally if they need to.

Often at this stage of the sales process, the sales team hand their clients over to Operations to deliver the solution. However, if you are going to maintain a long-term relationship with your client, potentially gain further business from them or even acquire referrals from them, make sure you personally stay in touch. Even an email a couple of days later to check in and make sure they are satisfied with the delivery or implementation of the sale will maintain their belief in you, your product and your company.

Sales secret

◆ Abandon a client at your peril. Only by maintaining customer contact can you ensure you are continuing to fulfil their expectations, build long-term relationships and gain referrals long into the future.

But what if the client won't commit? Then you need to know how to …

9

Overcome

VERY OCCASIONALLY YOU WILL come across a buyer (or a situation) that does not fit into the mould. They may have answered your questions previously and led you to believe they were preparing to make a commitment; or you may have missed something, or mistimed your close. Either way you may be faced with a situation where the buyer has not given, or is unwilling to give, their commitment.

Gaining the client's commitment

All is not lost. It is possible to still move forward and gain the client's commitment, but as you will have lost some rapport you will need to tread carefully in order to avoid alienating the client further.

Here is a checklist to run through in your mind should this situation occur.

Do you have rapport?

If you have not yet asked for the business but the client is showing no positive buying signals, then you may simply need to backtrack a step or two. Start by ensuring you are actively building rapport: follow their body language and voice signals, and use open questions to draw them into a conversation.

> *Sales secret*
>
> ◆ Sometimes a client's lack of engagement has nothing to do with you and everything to do with their own levels of self-confidence. They themselves could be feeling completely out of their own comfort zone.

If they are slow to engage with you, be patient: it could be that they simply need time to feel confident in your presence, particularly if you ooze self-confidence from every pore of your body. You may have inadvertently intimidated them. I know I have done this on occasion in the past. I have a very effervescent bubbly personality and sometimes when I meet people for the first time, I come bounding into their office like a Tigger and they have simply not been prepared for my levels of energy. It's interesting that I find that this happens more with women than men. So when I'm preparing to meet someone for the first time I make a conscious effort to make sure I Match and Mirror the other person's energy levels as well as the other rapport-building cues.

Remember to keep actively building rapport until the client demonstrates Pace and Lead. Even if they appear very reticent and distant, they can open up in a matter of seconds if you Match and Mirror them.

Have you qualified them correctly?

This is another classic error, thinking that you've qualified them sufficiently, yet it is only when you move further through the sales process that they begin to demonstrate signs that they are losing commitment. In which case, keep on asking questions. If you need to point out your confusion then *politely* ask them to re-qualify some areas where you are unclear.

> *'I must have got myself mixed up. Tell me again, what would be your ideal outcome? Why is that so important?'*

Have they told you the truth?

This is one outcome that is difficult to pre-empt, but sometimes the buyer will not answer your initial questions truthfully. Unless they are a barefaced liar, which is rare, it is more likely they have given you answers of how they *wish* their circumstances were, particularly when it comes to clarifying authority, budgets and resources, which has now meant they have come unstuck when you've progressed to gaining their commitment.

In this situation, again go back to re-qualifying them: except, this time make them aware that you can only help find them a solution if they give you accurate information.

> *'I'm confused. When I asked you previously about the next steps in moving ahead you said that you were looking to make a decision quickly and that you were in a position to make that decision. Therefore can you help me understand what is making you want to refer to your director before making a commitment? Am I missing something?'*

You've presented benefits that don't fulfil their emotional needs

It's possible that you've presented benefits that don't match their emotional needs, or it's also possible that you've fallen into the trap of presenting features without any benefits at all! In which case, use a couple of Compelling Statements where the benefits match the client's needs and then follow up with a test close to ensure they are received warmly. If the buyer is still not showing any buying signs, check through some of the other alternatives in this section to make sure there is nothing else you are missing.

They've already made a commitment to another supplier but don't want to tell you

Again, it is possible to uncover any other reason that could cause resistance in the sale by re-qualifying them. To avoid this situation occurring, a great question to ask is my old favourite:

> *'Is there anything else that is important for me to understand, that could prevent us working together, before we move ahead?'*

They don't feel any emotional reason to make a commitment right now

If the client doesn't perceive a sense of loss they will feel no urgency into making a commitment right now, so although they may agree with your proposition they will avoid making a commitment that requires immediate action or taking a risk now. Therefore it's important that when you present your proposition you build in a sense of urgency. There are other ways in which you can encourage the client to commit now.

◆ **Limited supply**. If your solution is in short supply then the client will need to make a decision quickly.

◆ **Reduced prices**. This is the technique that the retail industry uses when they reduce their prices in a 'sale'. By reducing their prices for a limited time, we as consumers are educated to believe we can grab a bargain. Remember if you discount your prices it must be either for a limited time or to close a particular deal.

◆ **Added value**. Offer the client additional product or services, thus increasing the value of their package but only if they are prepared to make a commitment now.

◆ **Favourable payment terms**. If this is a feasible option and you link it to gaining commitment NOW, then use favourable payment terms as a way of ensuring the client makes a commitment.

8-Step guide to handling objections

If there are any other reasons that the buyer is resisting and you are unclear about them, then use the 8-Step Guide to Handling Objections which will not only uncover any other objections but also demonstrate how you can overcome them.

About 15 years ago, I had a Manager once say to me 'Nicola, you're not very good at closing are you?' At the time I had hundreds of potential sales in my pipeline and, despite the fact that this was a rubbish thing to say to any salesperson as it would erode their confidence, I realised when I analysed my figures that he was right!

However, when I drilled down further to look at myself, my skills and my strategy, I actually realised that it wasn't that I was lacking in closing skills, it was that I didn't have a clue what to do next if the client said 'No': so rather than ask for the business and not know how to handle the objections, I avoided asking for the business! My best hope was that at some point in the sales processes they would actually ask *me* to place the order.

I decided to put my nose to the grindstone and got to work getting better in this particular area of my sales performance. I read every piece of material I could get my hands on regarding Objection Handling; I shadowed some super-salespeople to see how they did it and I put myself through training programmes that helped me with some new ideas. I then refined my own technique and over the years have developed the following 8-Step Guide to Handling Objections.

The amazing thing is that, after I had perfected this skill and added it to my sales skill toolbox ready to be pulled out when needed, I find myself very rarely (probably only two to five sales presentations a year) having to use it! By mastering this area of weakness, my confidence went through the roof and I felt comfortable asking for the business; and remember, if you don't ask you don't get. So by following all the previous steps and examples, I found that using this technique really *really* was the final step in gaining the client's commitment.

I suggest that you learn this skill as a script, perhaps pinning it on to your noticeboard or somewhere you can see it constantly, at least until you are confident you have mastered the structure and the phrases; then tear it up and throw the paper away. By then you can use your own language and style but still follow the same flow in the conversation.

Here are the 8 steps laid out as a flow chart. For a printable version go to **www.auroratraining.com**.

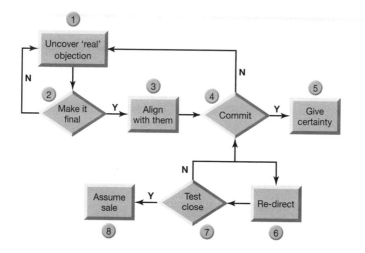

As you can see from the flow chart, the objection-handling process is almost a mini-sales process within the overall sales structure; however, it includes a few additional steps, so let's work through each step and I'll give examples of the language to use.

1. Uncover the real objection

The first stage in handling the buyer's objection is to be very clear about their *real* reasons for resisting your proposition, bearing in mind that up to this point they may not have been truthful, and all your attempts to fulfil their needs have been met with lukewarm responses. If all your previous attempts to build conviction and compel them to buy have failed, then it may be time to dig even deeper, particularly if they've given you a fob-off or a lame 'I'm not quite sure' or a 'Let me think about it'.

> *'I know you have reasons for saying that; do you mind if I ask what they are?'*

It's highly unlikely they will say 'No' to this question: they are much more likely to give you an opinion. However, before you begin to deal with this objection you need to ...

2. Make it final

There is no point handling this first objection only to discover that others are lurking below the surface. It is much easier to get them *all* out in the open, and then deal with them all in one go.

> *'Is that the only reason you are not able to move ahead right now?'*

Now clearly if they say 'No' to this question, revert back to the first question 'I know you've got reasons for saying *that*; do you mind if I ask what *they* are?' Keep going until all the objections are on the table and they say 'Yes'. At which point you now need to ...

3. Align with them

Aligning with your buyer is an important stage of the objection-handling process, as by simply stating the objection in the first place they have effectively misaligned with you. They have demonstrated that they do not agree with your point of view and are taking a different stance on the matter that is being discussed. Therefore, there is absolutely no point in continuing to add Compelling Statements and dishing out more benefits until the buyer is 'open' to receiving more information.

Unless you take the time to align with them, the only way you will ever win the sale is if they back down. Effectively when they object they are saying 'I'm right and you are wrong', and in this situation you can only ever overcome the objection if they were to admit that they were wrong and you were in fact right – something that the buyer's ego is unlikely to allow them to do. So by aligning with them at this stage you are, in effect, giving them permission to have a difference of opinion.

'I understand that this may feel like a big commitment.'

'I appreciate that I'm asking you to take a leap of faith.'

Or my favourite:

'That's great.'

By stating 'that's great' it makes them feel that you appreciate, understand and empathise with their point of view. When I align with someone, before moving further through the objection-handling structure, I can see clients visibly relax. It's almost as if they have been geared up for a fight and you can literally see their shoulders and face relax as they think 'That's great, they're not going to manipulate me, and they take my point of view seriously'.

Now you have aligned with them and enabled them to drop their barriers again and feel more comfortable with you, it's time to . . .

4. Gain their commitment to proceed together and find a solution to the objection

Quite simply, use a tie-down at this point that will ensure they are committed to moving forward in the sales process with you. There is no point in finding a creative way to handle their concerns if they are still not prepared to make a commitment.

> *'If we could find a way to handle that, you'd want to go ahead?'*

If they say 'No' to this question, then they are concealing a further objection that you will need to entice out of them by reverting back to the beginning. It's more likely, however, they will say 'Yes': they have no reason not to. Instead they will be thinking about how you can handle their objection.

Remember that some buyers are naturally more cautious than others and need to feel comfortable that the risk they are about to take is justified, therefore next . . .

5. Give them certainty

Before we build more emotional reasons and benefits to buy we want to ensure that we make the buyer feel comfortable with the risk we are asking them to take. Again a great way to do this is by using another client's testimony; however, make sure you link it directly to how this buyer is feeling at this moment.

A great way to structure this is to use the Feel, Felt, Found technique.

> *'I know exactly how you feel.'*

'I had another client who <u>felt</u> exactly the same way, when they were just where you are now.'

'What they <u>found</u> after they'd made the commitment was . . .'

And obviously share a positive story about someone else receiving the same benefits that this client needs.

So by now, the client should have relaxed once again; you should be very clear about their reasons for resistance, and you have their commitment that if you overcome their objection they will make a commitment. The next crucial stage in the process is to . . .

6. Redirect the objection

The only way you can ever truly overcome an objection is to turn it into a question that you can answer. Right now their mind is focused on the objection and all of their reasons for not wanting to buy. By using questions we can redirect the buyer's focus once again to the possibility of agreeing to your sales proposition.

'And that brings up a question. How can we make this <u>right for you?</u> Isn't it true that in spite of the (objection) *that you will benefit from* (list a feature), *which means* (state a benefit), *which really means* (state a further emotional benefit) *to you, and you will avoid* (wound, wound, wound).'

Don't pause and wait for an answer after the first phrase 'that brings up a question'. Using this language prompts their mind to open, evaluating the embedded question 'How can we make this right for you?' Again don't wait for a response, but this statement plants the seed in their brain that this *could* be right for them. It opens a loop.

Follow this up with a variation of your Compelling Statement where you state further features, benefits and emotional benefits which match their Hot Button, or further needs, wants and wounds you may have uncovered as you continued your conversation. Also, you may find you want to add in some pain avoidance into your Compelling Statement by stating the potential wounds that the client will want to avoid.

> *'And that brings up a question. How can we make this right for you? Isn't it true that in spite of the initial outlay, that by committing to this programme, in the time we will spend with your team they will leave feeling totally buzzed up and focused on delivering exceptional levels of customer service, which means that the customers in your local geographical catchment will always want to choose you first for all their pharmaceutical needs, which means that you will create the footfall necessary to achieve your targets, which means you won't have to worry about* not *achieving your sales figures or having sufficient revenue to fulfil your financial obligations, and isn't it true that despite the cost of this programme that the value will be recouped almost immediately, whereas the cost of not doing it . . . could be massive?'*

If you are going to change your proposition and either add further value or reduce the price, this would be the structure to introduce this new proposition, as you have already clarified that they are willing and able to move ahead, *providing* you handle the objection.

Just as you would after a normal Compelling Statement, it's necessary to ...

7. Test close

By test closing you will be able to read your buyer and understand how your latest solution has been received.

'Now, how does that solution feel?'

If they are still showing no signs of warming up, either build their conviction with a further Compelling Statement, or go back to step 4 gaining commitment. If they were to respond negatively to this, clearly they are throwing you curve balls and have not yet revealed their true reasons for not buying.

However, assuming the buyer responds positively and their buying signals are good then ...

8. Assume the sale

Hurray! Just as you would do normally, you have negated the previous objection, brought them round to your beliefs and way of thinking and they have realigned with you, in which case assume the sale. Ding!

'Fantastic. That's all sorted now. What will happen next is ...'

Sales secret

◆ Even the best salesperson on the planet won't win every sale every time. Learn from the sales you don't make so that you constantly improve next time.

We ring a bell in our office every time we make a sale and we love to hear the sound of that ding! We also have a dance we do to the sound of the credit-card machine. So we all love it when our days are full of **dinging** and **dancing**!

PART 3

Your *sales strategy*

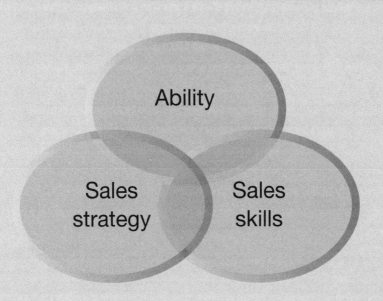

Sales strategy

- Generating opportunities
- Your ongoing recipe for success
- Avoiding the most common mistakes

The final part to uncovering sales secrets is knowing how to apply all of these newly acquired skills and knowledge. You could be the most confident and skilled salesperson in your field, but if your sales systems do not support your ongoing success, not only will you be frustrated, delivering results well below your potential but you'll also be likely to have a raft of dissatisfied clients and an overall poor reputation for customer service.

Your sales strategy needs to support two main outcomes: generate an ongoing supply of qualified opportunities, as well as identify, measure and manage your ongoing success. Throughout the next few chapters I will present a number of ways in which to do this. Not all will be relevant to your circumstances, market opportunity or business model, so draw from the pages the models that can add value and support you on your continued journey to success.

10

Generating opportunities

SITTING IN A SILENT OFFICE waiting for the phone to ring is not a strategy for success – it's a guaranteed strategy for failure! You may or may not have the support of a marketing team: however, even in your role as a sales professional you need to have multiple ways of seeking out and connecting with your ideal customer, and from there generating a steady stream of opportunities.

Maximising your existing client base

Before you start to spend budgets, time and resources generating new leads through traditional forms of marketing, I suggest you ensure you have maximised every potential opportunity that exists within your own client base and past sales activity.

I class customers into the following five categories.

1 Raving fans
2 Seasonal buyers

3 Spot purchasers

4 Customers with awareness

5 Customers with no awareness

Raving fans: Raving fans are great. They are your ideal customers for lots of reasons. These are the people who buy regularly from you and who rave about your services. They actively recommend you and have a huge amount of loyalty towards you, your services and your company. As well as being positive they are also ideal as they provide solid ongoing gross profit into your business. They may be on a contract with you for which they pay a monthly service charge, or you may have negotiated a long-term contract with them and they pay you a regular retainer. Raving fans allow you to forecast the cash flow of your business and predict your sales based on their orders.

Seasonal buyers: These customers are similar to the raving fans in that they are loyal to you and recommend your services but they only buy from you when a need arises, which can be difficult to predict. Their need may be only seasonal arising at certain points throughout the calendar year, or your product is not a consumable need which requires replacing regularly. So, for example, the company that supplies my office stationery could label my custom as a category 2: seasonal buyer; they know that when the need arises and I need to replace the toners in our printers, for example, we will place an order with them, yet they will not be able to predict when that will be.

Spot purchase: Spot purchasers are the category of customers who have only bought once. This could be, as the name suggests, because they made a buying decision on the 'spot'. Perhaps your services only require a one-time purchase or, for a whole other raft of other reasons, they have bought once and not returned. This may also represent customers who have engaged with you once, originally with the intention of using your product again, yet perhaps they have been let down, or the delivery of your services has fallen short of their expectations.

Potential customers with awareness: This category represents all the potential customers who have an awareness of you or your company but have not yet made a purchase. Perhaps you met at a networking event and swapped business cards, so you have their details and they have yours, but they have not yet purchased. It may represent all the potential customers who have seen your advert, read about you in the press, registered on your website, or someone has mentioned your company name to them, but for whatever reason they have not yet engaged with your company.

It may be that they do not fulfil your ideal customer criteria and do not yet have a qualified need for your services; it could be that they are loyal to another supplier. It could be that they need time for their opportunity to mature; they could be tied into an existing contract with another provider, or their new budget does not become available for a further six months. Yet despite all of these reasons, you are known to them.

Potential customers with no awareness: This final category represents the 'rest of the world' – everybody else who doesn't even
know that you and your company exist. Depending on the consumer awareness of your brand and your ideal customer this
may be a huge number. If you take a look at the blue-chip
brands in the world such as Coca-Cola, Nike, Microsoft, Disney
and MacDonald's amongst others, there are not many places in
the western world or even some parts of the developing world
where consumers are completely unaware of these brands.
Having said that, depending on the services you offer, you may
not need everybody in the world knowing who you are, providing that your potential ideal customers have heard of you.

Sales secret

◆ Use software that allows you to personalise any
communication you send out to customers, which makes
them feel more valued.

Turning customers with no awareness into raving fans

Whenever sales leads are fairly scarce, sellers start to panic
and begin to throw money, resources and efforts into their
marketing strategy. The focus shifts to the category 5 customers, the ones with no awareness. 'Quick we need to start
cold-calling', 'Hurry, let's run an ad campaign' or 'we need to
get some leaflets out fast'. However, these often present the
most expensive customers to target. I *always* suggest that,
before you start investing in expensive marketing campaigns,

you search closer to home and first ensure that you have maximised every potential opportunity that exists within your own client base.

So how can you improve your lead generation from your existing client base? The first stage is to ensure that you have correctly labelled all your existing customers, no matter what client-recording system you use. (I will cover how to keep accurate customer records in the next chapter.) I have a field on my customer database with a drop-down list of the five categories and ensure that every customer is labelled accordingly. That way if I want to run an offer to our existing seasonal customers I can easily market directly to them. Or perhaps I want to gain some new appointments with some of our category 4s: potential customers with awareness, who are likely to respond more positively than cold customers with no awareness at all.

So, for example, if I speak at a corporate event and delegates give me their business cards, all their details will be loaded on to our system and they will automatically be categorised as category 4 – awareness. They know of me and our business, they have some awareness; they've heard me speak, but they've not yet purchased any of our corporate services. However, the person who booked me for the event will be down as category 3 – spot purchase or perhaps even higher, depending on whether they have bought one service or a whole range of services.

After you've broken down your client base, the next stage is to ensure that you grow every potential opportunity. Rather than focus on one overall marketing strategy, a one-size-fits-all approach for all clients in the mix, decide how you can move the clients in each category further up the scale.

Turning seasonal buyers into raving fans

Do you need to take a look at your sales proposition? Do you offer a service that can be bought regularly? If not, could you introduce one?

Perhaps you could analyse the overall yearly spend of all your category 2 customers and encourage them to take out a yearly contract and to break their spend down into monthly payments, then send them a quarterly statement which analyses if they are over or under their allowance. This is the strategy that most of the utility suppliers in the UK use. You set up a direct-debit payment based on your estimated future spend, then each quarter your bill will show you the value of the services you have used against your accumulated payments. Then if needs be, you can adjust your payment schedule accordingly.

The firm that handles my personal and business accountancy needs uses this approach with their services and I think it's brilliant. Rather than invoice retrospectively every time I use their services, of which my needs for accountancy services are weighted to the one quarter of the year when my companies' financial year ends fall, they estimate all the services I will need throughout the year and break it down into a monthly payment. This helps me to cash-flow my businesses; it helps them forecast their own sales results and it also ties me in for another full year using their company and their services – genius!

Perhaps you need to introduce a subscription-based service that offers additional value to your existing seasonal buyers, so by paying for an additional monthly service, or by spreading their existing payments, they will either insure against a potential problem or gain some additional benefits from your company. Maybe you could offer a discount for buying services in advance or use retail offers such a 'Buy one get one free' to increase the sales volume. Could they join a voucher scheme that could be redeemed over a period of time?

When you consider the possibilities, there are lots of ways you could create more raving fans from your seasonal buyers; it may just mean re-looking at your sales proposition.

Turning spot buyers into seasonal buyers

Again, have customers purchased your services just once, as that is all your business model allows for, or is there another reason? If your product really truly is a spot purchase then perhaps you need to ensure it is placed in a way, either in retail or on your website, that entices many more customers to keep making spot buys.

However, have they purchased only once because they were dissatisfied in some way, or has someone else, a competitor, enticed them away? Perhaps you could offer an introductory offer to entice them back, or again you may need to look at your service and/or product proposition to allow them the opportunity to keep buying.

If you believe you may have lost customers because of poor service, then you will need to rebuild some trust. Pick up the phone and ask them. Don't faff around if you know you've let them down; just be honest: 'I'm giving you a call because I have a feeling that we may have fallen short of your expectations: therefore I would like the opportunity to rebuild your faith in our company.' Very often you can create an even more loyal long-term customer relationships based on how you handle a customer when they are dissatisfied with your services. Make them feel valued, show them you care, take it personally and they will reward you with more business.

Either way the best option is to communicate directly with your customers and ask what they need. If you have a particularly large client base this could be in the form of a survey; otherwise, pick up the phone or buy them a coffee and ask.

I designed and launched my Executive Coaching Programme based on a conversation I had with an existing customer, which was along the lines of 'Nicola, we've bought and benefited from every service you have but what's next? I want more.' I asked 'What other services could I offer that you would be prepared to pay for?', to which my client replied 'Exactly this, the opportunity to meet up once in a while and chat about my business and any ongoing problems – I would pay to have your advice and opinion.' Although I had the idea for this kind of service at the back of my mind, this particular conversation confirmed that I already had customers within my client base who would be ideal customers for this service if I introduced it.

Turning awareness into purchases

This category often presents the biggest opportunity for most salespeople; it is untapped sales opportunities waiting to be discovered. Over a period of time you may meet thousands of people, yet, because they are not a ripe opportunity, you shelve the client details and do nothing to mature the client into a real opportunity. At best you may enter their details on to a database; at worst you throw their details into a drawer. Sometimes you may even have clients who buy from you regularly, particularly in retail, where you know nothing about them and, because you haven't data captured their details, have no way of contacting them again.

I recently delivered a training programme to a group of financial industry professionals and when I asked them what they would do if they met someone, asked them when their mortgage was up for renewal and found out it was a few years away, I had one delegate boldly state 'Bin them!' Needless to say, that's why he was on my training programme!

You need to keep a record of every potential customer you meet, particularly in the business-to-business sectors, and then find a way of communicating directly with them in this category. Remember you have the advantage that they will know you, perhaps have even met you personally, so they are much more likely to be open to your sales advances than if you were contacting them cold.

I once consulted for a small local charity. When I arrived they outlined their plans to increase sales by taking space in a large shopping centre and offering a car-prize draw in return for signing up as a committed giver for their charity. A very expensive exercise to undertake. However, when we analysed their database they had over 10,000 clients who had either been previous givers yet cancelled their subscriptions, or completed a subscription form yet never set up their standing orders. This represented a much greater opportunity, so I suggested that, before we paid out for the exhibition space, we got to work and hit the phones with a telemarketing campaign. Needless to say, we achieved the desired increased revenue in a shorter period of time through a much more efficient *and profitable* strategy.

Keep communicating with clients in this category to keep them ticking over until a more saleable opportunity arises. Send them regular newsletter updates; ask them to subscribe to a text-messaging service or to join your list of twitterers. Find multiple ways to build a relationship so that they begin to feel a loyalty towards you, even before they've bought anything from you.

Throughout my own sales career I have worked within lots of sales environments and business models. However, the ones that were by far the toughest were the companies that had a business model that required a high proportion of new business each month in order to hit the sales target. As a salesperson starting every month on zero and having to sell your way up can be exhausting, draining and very very tough. This type of business model, which is often used by new and smaller businesses, means you are reluctant to take any time off as 2-weeks' leave in a month will likely mean you will miss that month's target – and if your livelihood depends on those figures, that's when you observe people working night and day on their businesses. This may be a requirement when you first start up, but it's not a long-term strategy for positive health and life balance, never mind long-term business success.

Therefore use the model above to find multiple ways to develop a repeat business model with every customer. It's a great feeling beginning your monthly sales target knowing that 70% of your sales target is already taken care of from your category 1, raving fans, leaving you time and resource to focus on acquiring the additional 30% from new business, whilst ensuring the quality of the delivery to your existing clients.

I have no existing client base to work with

However, if you have no existing client base – perhaps you are just starting your own business or you are entering a new industry or geographical area – you will need some traditional forms of marketing to generate your initial sales leads.

Although this is not a book focused on marketing strategies, here is a comprehensive list of all of the available ways to generate completely new leads. Ask yourself which, if any, methods you currently use.

Advertising	By placing an advert in traditional form either in publications, through the media or in public spaces in the form of billboards; or by advertising on websites that will attract your ideal customers.
Direct mail	By sending letters or leaflets (or perhaps a gift or quirky attention grabber) to a target audience.
Cold calling	By using telephony to contact prospective customers.
Networking	By attending organised business meetings or events with the purpose of meeting potential clients.
Free seminars	By hosting and then inviting potential clients to a free information seminar.
Public speaking	By speaking at an event or gathering where you are able to promote your services.
Exhibiting	By taking space at an organised event which attracts a footfall of your ideal clientele.
Sponsorship	Where your company name, slogan or brand is made visible to a large target audience through sponsorship of an event, other company or person.

Referrals	Where existing clients recommend your services to new potential clients.
Sign posting	Similar to referrals, other than it is made not by customers but by other individuals who are not your target audience but who are able to point customers in your direction. For example, a high street bank may point a customer in the direction of an accountancy firm, or a business support agency may recommend your mentoring services to a new potential client.
PR	By receiving coverage in press publications.
Internet	Through the use of your website, email marketing, online social networking, web advertising and online PR.
Clustering	Where you cluster with other suppliers who are not in direct competition but target the same ideal customer. For example, a wedding venue may recommend the services of a florist to a budding bride, or a car garage may recommend a tyre supply retailer. If a number of suppliers come together and target the same customer, then they are clustering.

The first stage in analysing your effectiveness in acquiring new business leads is to ensure that you monitor the effectiveness of any marketing activities you undertake. I suggest you have a field on your client database for 'source', where you can periodically analyse the results from your marketing strategy.

Your goal here should be two-fold: first to map out your most efficient sales process which you can easily duplicate, and secondly to ensure that you only ever spend money on marketing activities that will bear fruit. If you discover that advertising in the traditional sense, for example, does not generate any new leads for you, then when you receive a phone call into your office offering you a vastly discounted advertising space, no matter how good the deal, you will not be tempted to waste your resources.

Use the template below to record your past marketing methods and measure their effectiveness before deciding if you should stop/start or continue the activity, and then list any actions you should take as a result of your observations.

Method	Frequency	Effectiveness (high/medium/ low)	Should we (start/stop/ continue)	Actions

Ultimately you can only grow your sales by selling more or selling to more people. So when seeking out more people to sell to, ask yourself how you can spend more time in front of your ideal customer. If that means finding out where they buy their morning coffee on their way into the office and positioning yourself in the queue just in front of them, or buying them their coffee and handing it to them as they walk into work, then do it! Why not take cakes in for the reception-ist or write a 'No.1' in the corner of your business card if you have to wait in line to see the buyer (a tip from my friend Kate who used to be a pharmaceutical sales rep, who spent much of her professional life waiting in doctors' surgeries) so that your name is called first. You cannot sell if you cannot get in front of people. Use the principles of the Punchy Prologue, be creative, be memorable and be distinctive.

I once worked with a man called Ric Renton who was (and still is!) a bit of a character and who had become increasingly frustrated that he couldn't get an appointment with a particular managing director of a target company that he was aiming for. So he meticulously packaged up a kumquat into a beautiful gift box and sent it through the mail to the MD. Inside the note read 'I told your PA I would give my right testicle for an appointment in your diary, so here it is!' The next day he had the MD on the phone in fits of laughter, saying he had never had a salesman use such a uniquely distinctive and bold approach. Needless to say Ric got the appointment and the business that followed. Perhaps Ric's tactic may seem a tad bold for your personality but if you've nothing to lose, then go for it.

Gaining referrals

One of the easiest ways to grow your customer base and acquire new leads is to simply ask your existing clientele to recommend some new customers. If you provide a great service, you should find that some Raving Fans will naturally recommend you. However, you should also consider ways to actively seek referrals.

Following the delivery of my services, I revisit all of my clients for a follow-up meeting. The desired outcomes of these meetings are three-fold: review and discuss the feedback from the delivery of our services, explore any further sales opportunities **and** gain some referrals. I book in these follow-up meetings at the point of agreeing the contract delivery schedule, so they are already in the customer's diary and there is no possibility they may get missed or forgotten about.

If, however, you are not able to go back for a follow-up meeting with your client then the next best time to ask for a referral is at the point of gaining commitment. At this stage of the sales process the client has just aligned with you and agreed with your beliefs and proposition, so one of the ways the client can feel more certain about the decision they have just made is by recommending their choice to others, and this makes it the perfect time to ask them to endorse you. Like everything else, asking for referrals is easy when you know how.

> *'Who else do you know that may benefit from a conversation with us? Could you give me three names?'*

The only reason someone would be reluctant to give you a referral is that they are concerned you will hard-sell to them, which will reflect badly on the person giving the referral. So if the client shows any reluctance at the first question, I address their concerns head-on.

> *'We acquire most of our new customers from recommendations, so I know that you may be worried that if you give me some contact names that I'll ring them straight up and hard-sell to them. So let me assure you I will simply ask them a few questions to understand if there is any benefit in continuing a conversation.'*

> *Sales secret*
>
> ◆ If you asked every one of your existing clients to
>   recommend three other potential customers and you
>   convert one out of those three referrals into a new client,
>   you will have instantly doubled the size of your client base.

Using new technology

Back in 1990 there were only 140 websites in existence in
the world and only 1% of these were commercial. By 2009
there are now over 185 million websites on the internet, and
these days – no matter what your industry or business
proposition – to be taken seriously, you need to have a
strong web presence.

Who could have predicted the explosion of the internet
and the effect that it would have on everyone's lives? Customers' buying habits are constantly adapting and
salespeople need to know how to stay ahead of the trends.
Salespeople were often considered experts, the people with
all the knowledge, and very often a buyer would meet them
simply to find out an answer to their problem. However,
since the availability of the internet and the ability to get
online almost anywhere and in a heartbeat to connect to a
worldwide knowledge base, very often a buyer who has done
their research will know about you, your business, your
competition and will be more informed than you!

As a result many of the more traditional forms of marketing such as direct mail and advertising are being left behind

and their presence has less and less impact as more and more customers turn to the internet as their first choice when researching a potential need they may have. Twenty years ago if you needed to source a supplier, you would most likely have turned to your network of friends, colleagues and associates for advice, as well as looking in an appropriate directory or the Yellow Pages. Today you are much more likely, in addition to asking your network of friends, colleagues and associates, to google the internet for some options. Who could have predicted that using the search engine Google would result in it becoming a new verb in the English language?

As well as opening up massive new potential for companies to reach customers at the far corners of the planet, the internet also now possesses some challenges, as everyone clambers to claim their spot at the top of the search engines. So here are some checkpoints to work through that will ensure you are maximising the use of this still relatively new form of marketing.

If you are not on the web, get on it

Even if you offer a simple service-based product to your local geographic area and have previously relied on your local Yellow Pages for your marketing, a simple 'brochure style' website that won't cost the earth will ensure you can at least be found on the web if someone is looking for you. If a potential customer can't find you, but finds your competition instead when they surf online, you may lose a sale before you're even aware of it.

Include a strong call to action

Unless you are offering a completely web-based offering and need people to make their entire buying decision and complete a purchase online, it is likely that you will be using your web presence as a way of giving potential clients the opportunity to find out a little bit about you before they take their enquiry further. Therefore make sure you have your company contact details on the bottom of every page or at least very visible in the contact information, and include a very clear 'call to action' on the bottom of every page 'Call this number now for more information', 'Click here to find out more', 'Send us your response', and so on. Remember part of our definition of selling from the Introduction: 'turning motivation into action'. Therefore, unless you encourage your prospects to take action in some way, you are simply educating them, not selling to them.

Make your presence known

Search engine optimisation or SEO is an entire field of expertise in itself; however, even if you are not able to employ the help of an expert that can improve your web rankings, you still need to ensure that people can find your website. There is absolutely no point being on the web if no one knows you are there. Here are a few tips that will help improve your search engine rankings.

◆ Ensure you include a comprehensive list of meta tags behind every page of your website and remember to include those key words that may also be easily misspelt by a potential client.

◆ Ensure the first paragraph on your home page includes the key words customers are likely to use when searching for your kind of product or service.

◆ Register your company address with Google Maps as Google always lists websites which are linked to Google maps above those that are not.

◆ Register with appropriate online directories, as again your company can appear above others who do not have a listing.

◆ Include other website links in your site. The more reputable the website, such as Wikipedia and Amazon, the more influence it will have in your rankings.

◆ Keep updating your website. Google ranks sites it considers to be 'live' over those that have not been touched in months.

Capture potential client details

If the goal is not to sell to people over the internet, and you are using your website as a brochure facility, find a way to capture data. People will part with their contact details if they are receiving value in return, so offer them what I call a 'hook' – something that gives value upfront but requires little or no risk. At the bare minimum find a way to encourage clients to sign up for an e-newsletter or to give you their name and email address in return for some useful free information. At least you can then add them on to your central database as a category 4, awareness customer, so that you can continue to communicate with them and warm up any potential opportunity they may have.

Make sure you talk benefits not just features

Just as when you were compiling your Compelling Statement, make sure that you include some clear benefits to your product or service. Obviously anyone browsing will be unqualified at this stage, so assume that the person browsing your website is your target audience and write your website accordingly.

Make it sticky

In his book *The Tipping Point*, Malcolm Gladwell talks about the Stickiness Factor that forms part of the ingredients of a social phenomenon. *Sticky* means something that is memorable, something you are likely to talk about and something you will want to come back to again and again. Think about how some YouTube videos can be viewed by millions of people worldwide in a matter of hours because their content sparks off a viral campaign. So what makes your website sticky? Why would people want to come back again and again? Periodically change the layout (or at the very least the information within it). Post new information, include a blog, in fact any reason to encourage people to come back again and again. The more times they are exposed to your company name, the more you increase your brand awareness. Very often an initial sale comes along when the timing is right and you want to ensure that when the need to purchase your product arises within a potential customer, your name and company are the ones they recall.

Get linked in

Right now there is an explosion of social networking sites. It is likely that some will disappear once their popularity fades (who can remember Friends Reunited from a few years back!) and others will replace them, but as with any marketing activity your aim is to spend more time in front of your potential customers. If that means you need a presence on Linked In, Ecademy, Facebook, Bebo, My Space, YouTube, Twitter or any of the other social networking sites, then get on board and get linked in. These sites can provide a great way of driving traffic to your own website, so make sure that your website links to all your available social networking accounts and vice versa.

Keep an eye on your competitors

Just as you would with traditional forms of marketing, keep your eyes peeled for any new web developments by your competitors. Sign up for Google Alerts on any companies you want to track (or even yourself). That way you will be sent daily updates of any new references that have appeared on the web that relate to those key words.

Sales secret

◆ Having no technical know-how is no excuse for botching up this area in your sales strategy. Today's customers expect to be communicated to in more varied ways, so either learn how to do it or employ the skills of an expert.

11

Your ongoing recipe for success

IN THIS FINAL CHAPTER on maximising your success, now that you have acquired a huge amount of new knowledge, we will seek new ways of applying it into an ongoing strategy that increases your productivity and improves your ongoing sales success.

In a sales environment which can often appear uncontrolled and chaotic, you need to ensure you know the magic ingredients in your actions that create your personal levels of success, so that you can reapply them and continue to refine them, in order to maintain your sales success long term.

When you bake a cake, you need to know all the correct ingredients and to use the right recipe if you want to make the same tasty cake over and over again. If you haphazardly throw all the ingredients together without paying much attention to the recipe, then it is unlikely you will be able to repeat your success. So many salespeople I've worked with create great success, but because they don't know the ingredients of that success or the methodology that created it, they are unable to duplicate the same levels of success again, putting their initial gains down to luck or simply a fluke!

Understanding your sales process

An exercise I always ask new clients to complete is to map out their existing sales process – something that very few of them have any awareness of, instead preferring to run around like a headless chicken and haphazardly landing sales here and there. Before you can refine your sales process you need to clearly define the recipe for baking your particular sale.

You need to understand how many networking events or phone calls you need to make to get how many appointments. Then how many appointments or sales presentations you need in order to gain how many sales. Or how much PR will drive traffic to your store or website, or how many phone calls will be generated from how many leaflets.

Here is an example of a sales process.

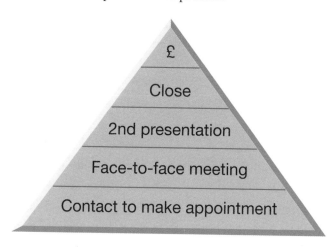

This is an example of a two-stage sales process, which is very often the case in business-to-business sales. In this example sales process, the salesperson must contact potential clients to make appointments. Then following an initial face-to-face meeting, return to make a more tailored and in-depth presentation which then leads to winning the business.

Your sales process may be similar to the above example or it may be vastly different. Perhaps you work in a purely tele-sales environment, or you have a particularly technical sell that requires multiple meetings, or you run a retail store that requires a certain level of footfall. Either way the first part in improving your success in this area is to map it out.

Increase your productivity or improve your conversions

As I've stated previously the only way to increase your sales is to sell more or sell to more people. Therefore you either need to increase your productivity and widen the width of the pyramid by increasing your lead generation and contacting more people, or by improving your conversions at each stage of the sales process.

One of the common mistakes that is made in measuring sales success is to measure just the end result – the value of the sales made – whereas it is as important to measure the conversions at every level of the sales journey. That way you may find that there is an obvious flaw in your sales process which can be easily improved: for example, can you reduce a three-stage sales process to two stages or a two-stage sales process into a one-call strategy? Or a poor conversion at one stage on the sales pyramid could highlight a weakness in a sales skill. For example, I have mentioned that I discovered I was weak at handling objections, and therefore not closing: I discovered this by analysing my own figures on my sales pyramid.

Sales secret

◆ Never close an appointment on a proposal, even if the client asks for one. Otherwise you will spend time and energy pouring your efforts into compiling a document that will sit unread on the buyer's desk. When you contact them to ask if they've read it, initially they will give you a polite fob-off and ask you to call back; however, after a while you become a nuisance and they will avoid any further contact with you. You have lost control of the sales process. Instead, close on a second meeting where you present your proposal. At the very least, agree a telephone meeting when you will discuss the proposal and email the document over a few minutes before the scheduled call.

Seeing your process laid out bare like this allows you to objectively see where you can make tweaks and changes to your recipe and then monitor the changes in your conversions when you adjust your strategy. Whenever sales results begin to fall, as a sales manager I always dig deeper and ask questions about activity; in fact I measure activity ongoing and develop KPIs (key performance indicators) that support our most effective sales model.

So if someone misses their sales target one week, they know the next question I will ask is 'How many phone calls have you made this week?' If you discover that your activity is high but your results are still poor, then perhaps you need to revisit your skill set. Are you properly building rapport, qualifying your clients or are you missing something even more fundamental in your market proposition which is putting buyers off?

When we map out a client's sales process like this, it's easy to see how a few tweaks here and there, a small increase, sometimes only 1%, in a particular conversion at a certain point on the pyramid can transfer into massive impact on the sales revenue at the top. What impact would improving your conversions by 5% all the way up the pyramid, or increasing your activity by 10% at the base have on your overall sales results?

The final area to measure on the pyramid is the average lead time it takes from sales opportunities to move from the bottom of the pyramid to the top. In some industries the average lead times can be as long as a couple of years, whereas in others it can be almost instant. Again, if you can shorten your lead times you will increase your overall sales results.

At the time of writing, here in the UK, we are in the grip of a recession and a world-wide credit crunch which has sucked the liquidity out of a number of industries. In these economic conditions the most subtle change I have detected in buyers' habits that most of my clients and indeed my own business are experiencing is that buyers are taking longer to make their decisions. People are still buying, but as so much fear has entered the marketplace, people are making much more considered decisions and are more risk-averse than they once were. So where

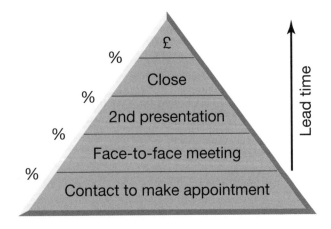

once an average lead time may have been 6 months, suddenly lead times for that same company are more likely to be 12 months or longer, and the businesses that have not noticed this change or been able to adapt to it are the ones that are struggling to turn a profit where once healthy margins used to exist.

> *Sales secret*
>
> ◆ Define your sales process and then develop a set of activity KPIs that work for you. That way if your sales results take a slight dip, providing your activity remains constant, you will be able to judge whether the drop in your sales results is a short-term blip, or an indication of a more serious change that may need closer attention.

Defining your own sales process

If you have absolutely no idea what your sales process is and you haven't got a clue how to start mapping it out, begin by recording all of your daily activity, then summarise your KPIs. Over time you will be able to map out a framework which you can begin to use as a template. Then ensure you record any changes to your recipe so that you can evaluate their effectiveness.

Ideally find a way to build this into your central client database; otherwise devise a template similar to the example below which you can use to record your figures manually. At the bare minimum keep a note in the corner of your diary of the number of appointments or phone calls you've made that day, so that you can manually collate the information.

Record any sales activity on a daily basis, breaking the categories down into the relevant activities for your business.

Remember 'what get's measured gets done' so any type of sales activity you undertake should be measured so that you can reflect on its effectiveness.

Alongside that, also record any tangible sales results you achieve throughout your working week. As well as recording new sales for the week, also record any new opportunities that enter the pipeline (even if at this stage the amounts are an estimate) and any sales that are lost.

Here is an example of an activity/sales report

Day of week	Activity Type	Number	Value of new pipeline opportunities	Value of sales lost	Value of sales closed
Monday	Cold calls First Appts. F/up Appts.	10 2 1	£16,000	£0	£0
Tuesday	Follow up Appts. Networking events	2 2	£2,500	£0	£1,500
Wednesday	Sales Calls (to f/up contacts made when networking) F/up telephone calls	50 15	£0	£2,000	£7,000
Thursday	Leaflets posted First Appts.	200 4	£14,250	£0	£0
Friday	Sales calls (to f/up leaflets) F/up sales calls to appts	120 5	£8,000	£4,000	£11,000

Weekly Summary
Activity

◆ Leaflets posted	200
◆ Networking events	2
◆ Cold calls	10
◆ Follow up sales telephone calls	185
◆ Face to face first appointments	6
◆ Face to face further appointments	3

Sales Revenue

◆ Pipeline Opportunities	£40,750
◆ Sales Lost	£6,000
◆ Sales Won	£19,500

Cumulative Sales Revenue YTD

◆ Total Pipeline Value	£464,00
◆ Sales Lost	£87,000
◆ Sales Won	£236,000

Remember that the sales you record in any given week may relate to sales activity from previous weeks, so you may not be able to draw any direct correlations from weekly activity to weekly sales revenue. However over time the figures will allow you to spot the patterns and convert your activity into percentages which will ensure you focus your efforts on your most productive sales activity and can spot any shift in your sales trends.

Unless you accurately record your sales activity, you are likely to fall into a very common salesperson's trap of believing that you are actually doing a lot more than is in fact the case.

> *Sales secret*
> ◆ Just because you are busy doesn't mean you are being effective. Make sure you focus on effective activities that drive sales results. Focus on increasing your activity and improving your conversions at each stage of the pyramid, and you can't fail to improve your sales revenue.

Increasing your basket value

If you are confident that you have maximised your sales process, your activity is high and your conversions are good, then your next avenue to explore that will increase your sales results is to increase the 'value' of each sale. The term 'basket value' comes from the retail industry where many companies measure not just sales revenue or number of sales, but also the average value of every customer's basket.

If you were to make the same number of sales, but increase the basket value by say 10%, you are guaranteed to increase your revenue and potentially your margins and profit too. One way to achieve this is obviously to increase your prices. Many companies (particularly service-based industries) tend to be reluctant to increase their prices on a yearly basis, yet, providing you are offering a value proposition, at the very least your prices should reflect the national change in inflation.

However, a better way to improve your average sale value is to up-sell a higher-priced proposition. This was the first kind of selling I was introduced to in the beginning of my career when I worked in American Express Business Travel Services. The sales opportunities came to me, as the phone would ring off the hook every day with clients needing flights, hotels, trains, cars and conferences booked as they travelled round the globe.

So although very often a client would outline their need and my job would be to simply organise the logistics to fulfil their requirement, very often we were incentivised to sell particular airlines, or hotel chains, which often cost the client more. So I needed to find ways to encourage my clients to switch airlines or upgrade their hotel room.

I always aimed to up-sell an Economy traveller to take a Premium Economy airline seat, or a Premium Economy traveller to upgrade to Business Class. Once they had experienced the better service they would very often ask for the higher-grade service the next time they booked – the pain of having to downgrade and travel with their knees up their nostrils again was too great – they would find a way to justify the additional cost ongoing.

So how could you now increase the average basket value in your sales? Are there add-on products or services you could sell? If not, why not develop some? Or can you up-sell to a higher-priced, but better-value proposition? Or is it simply time to increase your prices? Remember, people will buy if they believe there is value in the proposition? Use the techniques outlined in Part 2, particularly the Hot Button to uncover the real emotional need and then build your higher-value proposition based on that information.

Keep accurate records

I have mentioned a few times the importance of keeping accurate sales records, so now let's cover what you should and shouldn't be recording. Sales records shouldn't just record the client details once a sale has been made and your customer moves into the list of existing clients; you need to ensure that whatever system you choose it fulfils the following criteria:

◆ Maintains accurate customer data and contact details (including as much personal information as you deem necessary)

◆ A diary system to schedule follow-up activity

◆ A record of the sales history with details of previous contacts, telephone calls, associated documents and previous information sent

◆ It needs to be transparent so that other team members can pick up the thread in your absence or cross-reference the same client

◆ An easy way to analyse your sales statistics, including sales revenue vs target, pipeline sales and projected revenue, sales activity and sales process KPIs.

In the early part of my sales career, which was long before the advancement of many of the technologies we now take for granted, I travelled with all my customer records in a manual filing system in the boot of my car. I had a manual diary system for managing my time and scheduling follow-up calls and appointments, a manual record of my daily sales activity and every order was completed in triplicate: one copy for the customer, one for my records and one posted off to head office that evening to be processed the next day.

In today's world this all seems archaic and that's because it was! These days with the wide use of mobile phones, computer software and the internet, it's possible to complete all of these tasks on one system, which you can then synchronise with your electronic diary, which in turn synchronises with your mobile phone, and with one touch you have all the information you need at your fingertips. When used correctly these CRM (customer relationship management) systems can massively improve your productivity and ensure you don't miss any opportunities as you manage all of your sales relationships.

There are many software options widely available that can support every type of business and sales process; some are industry specific but even the 'off the shelf' packages include fields that can be easily customised with drop-down fields, allowing you to quickly collate analysis and get an instant snapshot of your or your team's performance. When bought off the shelf they are a very cost-effective option even for a small business and, providing you put the information in and use it every day to update all of your customer activity, it will help you keep on track with one push of a button.

Over my career I've used a raft of software systems including Galileo, Sabre, Saleslogix, Goldmine, and I currently use a package called Act in my business, which also has the advantage of linking directly to my accountancy software and my online marketing software as well. I particularly like the sales planning tools and pipeline reports which take the headaches out of manually collating all of the information I covered in the previous section.

Whatever system you use, be it manual or computer-based, the key is to improve your productivity, your sales conversions and your customer service experience. You should be aiming to input information only once. Duplication of complex systems will hinder your results and is more likely to be inaccurate.

Build the week

'Build the week' is the phrase I use to build up your productivity as your week progresses. A day in the life of a salesperson can include answering and handling a number of emails, dealing with some in-house queries, making a ton of sales calls both to existing and new clients, compiling and sending off some introductory letters or direct mailings, preparing a sales presentation, recording your sales activity, attending a breakfast network meeting – and that's before you travel to and from your scheduled face-to-face sales meetings for that day!

So it's easy to see that if you take your eye off the ball even for a moment, how easily the hours and days can slip by and suddenly you reach the end of your week and you haven't hit your target. By breaking your activity down into chunks that you schedule for certain times on certain days, you will be much more organised and ensure you still have sufficient time in your diary for activities that lead to sales.

This is particularly useful if you work in a small business and sales is not your only responsibility, or your role includes other activities other than just pure sales.

Build-the-week activities are broken down into the following four types:

Action	When you focus on sales-generating activities, such as phone calls, face-to-face meetings, attending networking events, and so on.
Focus	When you review your current sales results and plan your immediate activities.
Report	When you collate and briefly analyse your activities and sales figures.
Boost	When you plan in a sales activity that will boost your motivation, perhaps a phone call to a raving fan when you are fairly certain you will close a deal, or attend a final-sales presentation that you already feel fairly confident about.

Depending on the weekly schedule you work, plan in the different activities at a time that will increase your effectiveness. An example of a five-day working week is below.

	Monday	Tuesday	Wednesday	Thursday	Friday
AM	Focus Boost Action	Action	Action	Action	Action
PM	Action	Action	Action Report Focus	Action	Action Report Boost

On a Monday morning spend a few moments ensuring you are focused for the week ahead. You have completed any research you need to do for any appointments later in the week, you have all of your sales materials gathered together and you hit the ground running. I've always encouraged my sales teams to come in a bit earlier on a Monday morning to do their planning for the week and get ahead, and I'm happy to let them knock off early on a Friday, providing they've hit target, of course.

As sales is a very transparent industry and one that is easily measured, you should be rewarded on your results not your activity anyway, so even if your company won't pay you for any additional hours you put in, if it will help your overall results then it's a no-brainer for me. Personally I prefer to do my planning on a Sunday night, spending a few hours catching up on emails, preparing my 'sales bag' and basically getting my preparation out of the way for the week ahead.

After spending time planning, build a Boost activity into your morning. This is a sales phone call or meeting that will increase your confidence and give you that extra boost that helps to create upward spirals throughout the rest of your week. So if you are planning a repeat sales visit with a regular customer and you are expecting a repeat order, then schedule the appointment early on in your sales activity.

Continue with your sales action before regrouping halfway through your week. By the end of your working week, ensure you compile your reports, refocus for the following week and build in a further Boost activity that will carry your confidence over the weekend and ensure you start the following week on a high.

> *Sales secret*
>
> ◆ Aim to achieve your weekly sales target by midway
> through your week. That way by reporting and
> refocusing by Wednesday afternoon, if you have achieved
> your target then, you will smash it and 'bank' some
> additional sales by the end of the week; and if you
> haven't yet quite made it, then you still have time to
> review your activity so that you can catch up by Friday.

Sarah Miller is top saleswoman in her company and has been for the past 13 years. She sells tailor-made upmarket Caribbean holidays, so, although over the years she has developed a bank of loyal clients who always come to her first, so too have many of her colleagues within the company. So how does she do it – how has she maintained her position as top sales performer consistently for the past 13 years? Sarah is meticulous in breaking her week down into bite-size chunks, ensuring she maintains a laser-sharp focus on a daily basis. She breaks her sales targets down into personal daily targets before recording every single sale on a very visible scale that she can follow throughout the day. At the end of each day she views her position against her colleagues and can see if she is ahead or behind their performance. She is clearly motivated and very highly driven.

Very often by only making one or two recommendations to her clients that fulfil their needs even more so, yet increases their holiday price, sometimes by as little as 5%, Sarah makes sure she surpasses her targets – everyday. Obviously over a 12-month period this cumulates until she far surpasses her targets.

She recently took maternity leave, yet, by using this strategy, managed to hit her yearly sales target in the 9 months she worked before leaving to have her baby – something that some of her colleagues failed to do in the full 12-month calendar year.

And finally, now you have all the information you need to become super successful in selling, make sure you avoid some of the most common mistakes of other sales professionals.

12

Avoiding the most common mistakes

A WISE MAN ONCE SAID 'Why would you want to go through life and have to learn from all your own mistakes? Learn from and avoid making the mistakes everyone else has!'

Wise words indeed. By reading this book thus far you have discovered new ways to improve your own sales ability, learn some new sales skills and uncover new ways of applying them that will increase your sales results. So, in this last chapter I will briefly outline the most common mistakes that I come across in my sales consultancy and coaching practice. Although all the answers have already been covered, as I said right in the Introduction, knowledge without action is worthless. So as you read this list take a final look below and make sure you avoid repeating the most common mistakes that will erode your sales success.

Your sales ability

1 Low self-belief and poor confidence levels.

2 Taking rejection personally which, again, erodes confidence.

3 Inability to immediately bounce back after a rejection, which affects your next sales presentation.

4 Not wanting to be labelled as a 'salesperson', therefore avoid generating sales opportunities.

5 Not understanding the real reasons why people buy your product or service and therefore targeting the wrong ideal customer.

6 Not following up sales leads, instead allowing them to go off the boil.

7 Low motivation due to poorly defined personal goals.

Your sales skills

8 Low empathy skills, which leads to poor rapport.

9 Failing to effectively qualify opportunities and wasting time chasing 'dead' opportunities.

10 Presenting the opportunity before qualifying the Hot Button, simply because the client shows an initial interest.

11 Agreeing to send a proposal or brochure at the end of a meeting or telephone call and failing to agree the next steps.

12 Not gaining commitment by using tie-downs or test closes before moving the conversation on.

13 Presenting features and missing benefits altogether, or presenting benefits that do not match clients' needs.

14 Not asking for the business!!

Strategy

15 Not asking for referrals.

16 A lack of healthy competition within a sales team which can add motivation.

17 Poor sales management, and no accountability for activity and results within the individual team members: instead, they are left to run amok. Or a lack of self-discipline if you are responsible for your own accountability.

18 Broken promises – rewards and recognition that have been offered are not forthcoming, which demotivates the salesperson. Or not taking a break if you need to rejuvenate yourself.

19 Poor time management, not focusing on activities that deliver results, becoming sidetracked in less productive activities.

20 No idea of the company's sales process: instead, scrabbling, hitting and missing sales opportunities.

21 Not measuring activity KPIs: instead, only focusing on revenue generation.

22 Poor record-keeping and not accurately recording sales history.

23 A poor sales environment which does not inspire or motivate and you wouldn't want to work in.

24 Overcomplicated systems that pull resource away from sales-generating activity.

And finally, the biggest sales secret of all!

When compiling the content for this book, I asked everyone I know to tell me their one big secret – what was the one thing that they did that had the greatest impact on their overall sales success? As you will have read, many of the stories and examples made it into the book. However, absolutely everyone agreed on one massive sales secret that always has the biggest impact – *your attitude*!!

Maintaining a positive belief system and an empowering outlook will allow you to recover from setbacks, sets you apart from your competition and enables you to create phenomenal results over the long term. A positive attitude will always win out. It's easy to remain positive when things are going your way. However, very often our character, resilience and personal growth occurs when we are up against it and we face a challenge. It is in these moments that we need to pay particular attention to our mindset.

Everyone I have ever met who seems to have created an overnight success either personally or professionally and is basking in their rewards, usually has a back story that often involves long periods of struggle, hard work and maintaining a positive self-belief long before the rewards reflect their true effort.

Sales secret

◆ We can't always influence what happens to us – only how we choose to respond. We can always choose our attitude, so choose yours wisely!

Creating success in your sales is something you should feel proud about. Wear your salesperson's badge with pride and decide now to use these secrets to become the best salesperson you can be. You, your business and your customers will all reap the rewards.

So it's time now for you to take the same advice a mentor once said to me 'Nicola, stop talking about how good you are, or how good your results will be: instead, put your nose to the grindstone, your backside in the air, get to work and let your results speak for themselves.' Thank you Jeremy Taylor for those wise words.

If you would like more support, sign up for our FREE 30-day Secrets of Success in Selling Support Programme at **www.auroratraining.com** and we will send you more information, together with our bonus chapter on 'The 5 styles of successful selling'. Send your name and email address to **info@auroratraining.com** with 'Bonus Chapter' in the heading.

Want more?

Seminars, Keynote Presentations, Media Appearances, Consultancy, Coaching, Books & Audio Programmes

Do you need to inject some fire and passion into your team? Do you need an inspirational female speaker at your next business event? Are you seeking a topical opinion for your panel or magazine? Or would you like to find out how to come along to a seminar or join a vibrant on-line community? Then act now and find out more about the variety of services that Nicola and her team can offer.

Visit www.auroratraining.com
Telephone +44 1207 XXXXXX
Email: info@auroratraining.com

To be added to the free 'Northern Lights' online newsletter offering inspirational content and practical tips simply email the word 'newsletter' to **info@auroratraining.com**

Visit Nicola's individual companies online.

- Aurora Training at **www.auroratraining.com** for seminars, corporate training, consultancy and coaching.
- Nicola Cook at **www.nicolacook.com** for media appearances, keynote presentations and publication contributions.
- Aurora Foundation at **www.aurorafoundation.co.uk** for fundraising and work in the community.

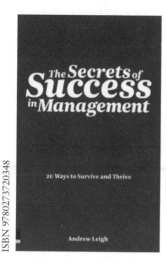

ISBN 9780273720348

Do you *want to be an ordinary or extraordinary manager?*

These are *real* secrets. Pearls of wisdom learnt through years of hard work leading and managing successful teams. They are what every established manager wishes they'd been told when they first started out.

Very few become the manager they truly set out to be – now *you* can.

Introduction

In my imagination, I have a film running through my head. In it, a new or recently appointed manager picks up *The Secrets of Success in Mangament* and experiences a tingle of excitement on realising "Hey! This is really useful stuff!"

The film continues with this person handing on the book to a colleague, urging "You have to read this, it's gold dust!" Well, that is my dream anyway. It is certainly meant to be the sort of book I wish I had found when starting as a manager—stuff I could use, as I struggled to turn on other people to do their best, to do what I wanted them to do.

You are on an exciting, creative and rewarding journey, becoming a successful manager. Like anyone embarking on a lengthy trip, it is worth taking some essentials with you.

While not exactly a manual of how to manage, consider *The Secrets of Success in Mangament* as more like a compass, or a reassuring traveller's kit to support you along the way…

Turn the page for a preview…

1

Cultivate emotional Intelligence

IN A TEAM MEETING, YOU NOTICE one of the normally articulate members doodling and looking glum. You could immediately call them on it. Instead, you wait until after the meeting and gently pull this person aside. Tactfully, without appearing to pry, you ask "You seemed unusually quiet in there, and I just wondered if anything is the matter?" That is when you discover this team member's wife has breast cancer. You not only feel sad and show it, you also urge them to take the rest of the week off, to be at home and support their wife during this difficult time.

Fighting back his tears, the team member thanks you profusely and says he will do that, promising first to finish his current assignment today. Finally, you ask whether he wants the other team members to know the situation and whether he will tell them or would like you to do so.

This example of emotional intelligence (EI) in action, helps explain why some managers thrive, while others mark time, or fail altogether. To succeed in your new role, you need to grasp the essence of EI, and keep developing yours throughout your career in management....

Soft is often the hardest

As its name implies, emotional intelligence is the ability to manage yourself and your emotions and relate to those of other people. These so-called soft skills are in fact the hardest to learn, as they do not come neatly packaged as a discrete set of techniques. Yet in explaining why people succeed in their job, they matter twice as much as conventional IQ or technical skills argues researcher and author Daniel Goleman, who helped put EI on the map.

So, how do you make sense of emotional intelligence? How can you make sure you have your fair share of it?...